Sweetie pie

Sweetie pie

Deliciously indulgent recipes for dessert pies, tarts and flans

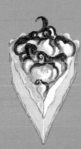

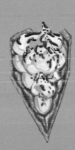

Hannah Miles

photography by Steve Painter

illustrations by Selina Snow

RYLAND PETERS & SMALL
LONDON • NEW YORK

For Poppy and Jemima,
two beautiful girls who love to bake

Design, photography and prop styling Steve Painter
Editor Kate Eddison
Production David Hearn
Art Director Leslie Harrington
Editorial Director Julia Charles
Publisher Cindy Richards

Food stylist Lucy McKelvie
Food stylist's assistant Cherry Ackerman
Indexer Hilary Bird

First published in 2015 by
Ryland Peters & Small
20–21 Jockey's Fields
London WC1R 4BW
and
519 Broadway, 5th Floor
New York, NY 10012

www.rylandpeters.com

10 9 8 7 6 5 4 3 2 1

Text © Hannah Miles 2015
Design and photographs © Ryland Peters & Small 2015

Printed in China

ISBN: 978-1-84975-610-5

A CIP record for this book is available from the British Library.
US Library of Congress CIP data has been applied for.

Notes
• All spoon and cup measurements are level unless otherwise specified.
• All eggs are medium (UK) or large (US), unless otherwise specified. Uncooked
or partially cooked eggs should not be served to the very old, frail, young
children, pregnant women or those with compromised immune systems.
• When a recipe calls for the grated zest of citrus fruit, buy unwaxed fruit and
wash well before using. If you can only find treated fruit, scrub well in warm
soapy water before using.
• Ovens should be preheated to the specified temperatures. We recommend
using an oven thermometer. If using a fan-assisted oven, adjust temperatures
according to the manufacturer's instructions.

contents

Introduction

One of my favourite three-letter words is PIE, and being asked to write this book made me very happy! However, if you ask me to tell you what a pie is, I have no straightforward answer for you, as pies come in many shapes and guises. Some encased in pastry with tangy fruit fillings, others creamy and indulgent with baked custards or piled high with whipped cream. What is certain is that nothing beats a homemade pie! Straight from the oven, bursting with berries or topped with cream and chocolate, there are fewer greater comfort foods than pie to dig into with friends.

If you asked someone in England to name a pie, I expect that it would be an apple or plum pie, but in America, while apple pie is, of course, a national dessert, there are many other popular pies such as Mississippi mud pie (said to resemble the Mississippi swamp base, but far more tasty!) and Key lime pie.

In addition to pies, this book also contains recipes for tarts. This is where the position becomes even more challenging; if there is confusion about the definition of a pie, trying to distinguish between pies and tarts is even more difficult. Some say it is determined by the shape of the dish that the dessert is cooked in, with pie dishes having sloping sides and tarts having straight sides. Others say that it is to do with whether there is a pastry top to cover the pie or not. I have even heard it said that pies are served hot, whereas tarts are served cold, but I do not subscribe to this notion! Whatever the difference, all recipes in this book make delicious desserts, whatever you want to call them, and probably no more explanation than that is needed.

The first chapter of this book is Classics – from traditional deep-dish apple, popular with a pretty pie funnel in the centre to allow the steam to escape, to one of my favourites, lemon meringue pie, topped with billowing meringue and filled with a tangy lemon custard. My mum makes the best lemon meringue pie, so this is a recipe very close to my heart.

The Fresh and Fruity chapter contains pies and tarts filled with every type of fruit – from the classic glazed fresh fruit tart, commonly displayed in the windows of fine Parisian patisseries, to more quirky flavours, such as grapefruit and mint (you will have to trust me that this flavour combination works!), and pineapple and star anise tatins with rich buttery caramel.

If it is indulgent pies and tarts that tickle your tastebuds, then look no further than the Rich and Indulgent chapter, where you will find delights such as hazelnut croquant pie, topped with shards of praline and clouds of cream, and chocolate fondant tarts, baked in rich chocolate cookie-crumb cases with a gooey molten centre. Also on offer are coffee pies – for a perfect pick-me-up when you need a caffeine hit – and a caramelized nut tart, laden with buttery caramel sauce.

The Family Treats chapter contains recipes with all your favourite candy bars and ice creams, from cookie dough pie – with a giant crisp cookie crust and soft cookie dough baked in a creamy custard – to treacle tart. The ice cream pie in this chapter is a great dessert to keep stored in the freezer for days when you need a dessert but don't feel like baking – it is topped with swirls of chocolate and chocolate confections, making it the perfect party pie!

For pies with a 'round the world' feeling, look no further than the Global chapter, which contains pies inspired by all of my favourite holiday destinations – why not let a piña colada pie transport you to sunny tropical beaches or, for a trip to the borders of Germany and France, enjoy the combination of bitter chocolate, sweet cherry and kirsch flavours of the classic Black Forest gateau in the form of an irresistible creamy pie.

Finally, for perfect Christmas, Hanukkah and Thanksgiving desserts, turn to the Holiday Specials chapter, and enjoy the delicious flavours of eggnog custard pie, mincemeat tarts or a twist on the classic apple pie made with cinnamon, cranberries and pears – delicious with lashings of hot custard sauce or cream.

Whatever the reason, whatever the season, get your pie pan out, don an apron and rustle up these simple but delicious pies and tarts for your friends and family.

Pastry success

Pastry can be intimidating, but it really doesn't need to be. The art of making good pastry is to keep everything as cold as possible. Cold hands, cold butter and a cool kitchen are essential. If your hands are naturally warm, simply run them under the cold tap or soak them in cold water before you start to make your pastry. Keep the butter in the refrigerator until just before using, and cut it into small cubes with a chilled knife to minimize the amount you need to handle it when rubbing it into the flour. For best results, it is also important to chill the pastry before rolling it out and then again once it is in the pan, as this will help prevent it from shrinking when it is baked.

Pastry is in fact simple, and a basic shortcrust pastry is made with regular storecupbord ingredients of just flour and butter. It can be made ahead and stored, wrapped in clingfilm/plastic wrap, in the refrigerator.

Basic shortcrust pastry

This basic pastry recipe is suitable for any of the recipes in this book that are made with shortcrust pastry. This has no sugar in it, and I find it works well with most sweet pies, as the fillings can often be sweet enough.

280 g/generous 2 cups plain/all-purpose flour
a pinch of salt
115 g/1 stick butter, chilled

Sift the flour into a large mixing bowl to remove any lumps, and add the salt. Cut the butter into small cubes using a knife. Dust your hands in a little flour, then, using your fingertips, rub the butter into the flour and salt, until it is the consistency of fine breadcrumbs.

Add 1–2 tablespoons cold water, and mix in with a round-bladed knife, adding a little more water if the mixture is too dry. Bring the dough together into a ball. It is important that you handle the pastry as little as possible for the best results.

Wrap the pastry in clingfilm/plastic wrap and chill in the refrigerator for 1 hour.

Sweet shortcrust pastry

Sweet shortcrust pastry is delicious: rich from the butter and egg yolks and sweet from the sugar. If you have a sweet tooth, you can use this pastry with any recipe in this book that calls for shortcrust pastry.

220 g/1⅔ cups plain/all-purpose flour
115 g/1 stick butter, chilled
60 g/5 tablespoons caster/granulated sugar
2 egg yolks

Sift the flour into a large mixing bowl to remove any lumps. Cut the butter into small cubes using a knife. Dust your hands in a little flour, then, using your fingertips, rub the butter into the flour, until it is the consistency of fine breadcrumbs.

Add the sugar and egg yolks, and mix in with a round-bladed knife, adding a little more water if the mixture is too dry. Bring the dough together into a ball. It is important that you handle the pastry as little as possible for the best results.

Wrap the pastry in clingfilm/plastic wrap and chill in the refrigerator for 1 hour.

Store-bought pastry

I have to say that I am not a purist when it comes to pastry and I know that sometimes people are short of time and need to rustle up a dessert quickly. On those occasions, it is absolutely fine to use store-bought pastry. These days, good-quality pastry is available from all supermarkets – both shortcrust and sweet shortcrust. Frozen ready-made pastry is also available, and is handy to keep in the freezer for when you have unexpected visitors. A 500-g/18-oz. pack of ready-made shortcrust pastry will be sufficient for any of the recipes in this book

Some of the recipes in this book are made with puff pastry. Made at home, puff pastry is really delicious, but it takes time to fold the leaves of pastry with layers of butter, as you need to chill it between each folding process. For the purposes of this book, the recipes using puff pastry are made using store-bought puff pastry. If possible, always select all-butter puff pastry, as it tastes delicious. If you wish to make your own puff pastry, there are plenty of recipes available online with step-by-step guides.

A few of the recipes in this book are made with filo/phyllo pastry. I always buy this. I attempted to make it on one occasion during MasterChef, but it was very difficult and I would not recommend it when perfectly good filo/phyllo pastry is available to buy – life is definitely too short to make your own filo/phyllo pastry, in my view!

Lining pans with pastry

The key to a good pie or tart made with pastry is to line the tart pan very carefully with your pastry, as it is important that the pastry is neither too thin nor too thick. When pastry is too thick, it detracts from the delicate nature of your pie filling; too thin and you risk the pastry cracking and the filling leaking under it while the pie is baking. You need to make

sure that you grease your pie dish or tart pan well, to ensure that the pastry does not stick and the baked pie or tart can be removed easily after it has cooked. I always use loose-bottom pans.

Dust a clean work surface liberally with flour. Remove the pastry from the refrigerator and allow it to come to room temperature for a few minutes, so that it is easier to roll. Dust the pastry ball and a rolling pin with a little flour, and roll the pastry out thinly using the rolling pin to about 2–3 mm/⅛ in. thickness and into a size just larger than the pan you are lining, allowing a few centimetres more than the size of your pan, to give sufficient pastry to come up the sides of your pan. To move the pastry, place the rolling pin in the centre of the pastry and fold one half of the pastry gently over the rolling pin. Place your pan next to the pastry, so that you do not have to lift the pastry too far. Lift up the pastry using the rolling pin and place it gently over the pan. Press the pastry in gently but firmly with your fingers and trim away any excess pastry using a sharp knife, but leave some pastry hanging over the edge of the pan – this will be trimmed neatly after the tart is baked. Place the pan on a baking sheet and chill in the refrigerator for a further 30 minutes. Your pie crust is then ready for baking.

Baking blind

'Baking blind' is the process of cooking a pastry case/pie shell before you fill it, to make sure that liquid fillings do not make the base of your dessert soggy. There is nothing worse than a pie with a soggy bottom!

Baking blind is a very easy process, as long as you have baking beans (small ceramic balls) with which you fill the pastry case to ensure that the pastry cooks evenly. This process also helps to prevent the sides of the pastry case from shrinking as you bake it. If you do not have baking beans, you can use uncooked dry rice grains, lentils or split peas. To bake blind, prepare your pastry case and preheat the oven to 200°C (400°F) Gas 6.

Line the pastry with baking parchment, fill with baking beans and bake blind in the centre of the preheated oven for about 15–20 minutes, until the pastry is golden brown and crisp. If you are preparing a pie that is not baked any further, cook the pastry case for a further 5–10 minutes, with the baking beans removed, until the pastry is completely crisp. For other pies which require further cooking, the pastry will continue to cook while the pie is cooking, so this additional baking is not needed.

Cookie-crumb pie crusts

As an alternative to using pastry as the crust for your pie or tart, many of the recipes in this book are made with a cookie-crumb pie crust. I love this type of crust, as they can add additional flavours to the desserts. They are quick and easy to prepare and do not require any additional baking. Cookie-crumb cases can be made with virtually any type of biscuit/cookie, so the possibilities are endless. My personal favourites are chocolate sandwich cookies, such as Oreos, as the cream filling and dark chocolate cookies make the perfect vanilla chocolate case.

As the recipes in this book call for different types and quantities of biscuit/cookie, you will need to use the quantity called for in your recipe and follow the basic instructions below.

Crush the biscuits to fine crumbs in a food processor or blender. If you do not have a food processor or a blender, do not worry; simply place the biscuits/cookies in a clean food bag with no holes and bash them to fine crumbs using a rolling pin. If you have not got a rolling pin to hand, just use a saucepan or any heavy kitchen object instead. I have even been known to use a can of baked beans when on holiday with limited kitchen resources!

Once you have your crumbs, melt the quantity of butter specified in your recipe, until just melted. Stir the melted butter into the crumbs and toss well with a spoon to ensure that all the crumbs are coated in the butter. Sometimes, depending on the texture of your crumbs, a little more or less butter may be needed. For this reason it is best to add most of the butter, but not all of it, and stir it into the crumbs, adding the rest of the butter gradually. You do not want the mixture to be wet, but it should stick together when you press it with a spoon. If the mixture is too crumbly, it will not make a firm pie crust, so you should add a little extra melted butter to achieve the correct consistency if needed.

To make the cookie-crumb pie crust, tip the buttery crumbs into the pan and press them down firmly with the back of a spoon, either just over the base of the pan or up the sides of the pan as well, depending on what your recipe calls for. To press the crumbs up the side of the pan, push the crumbs up from the base of the pan so that they go up the sides. The top of the crumbs on the side will be uneven. To neaten the top, simply press down around the top of the case with the spoon. Chill the case in the refrigerator if you do not need to fill it immediately.

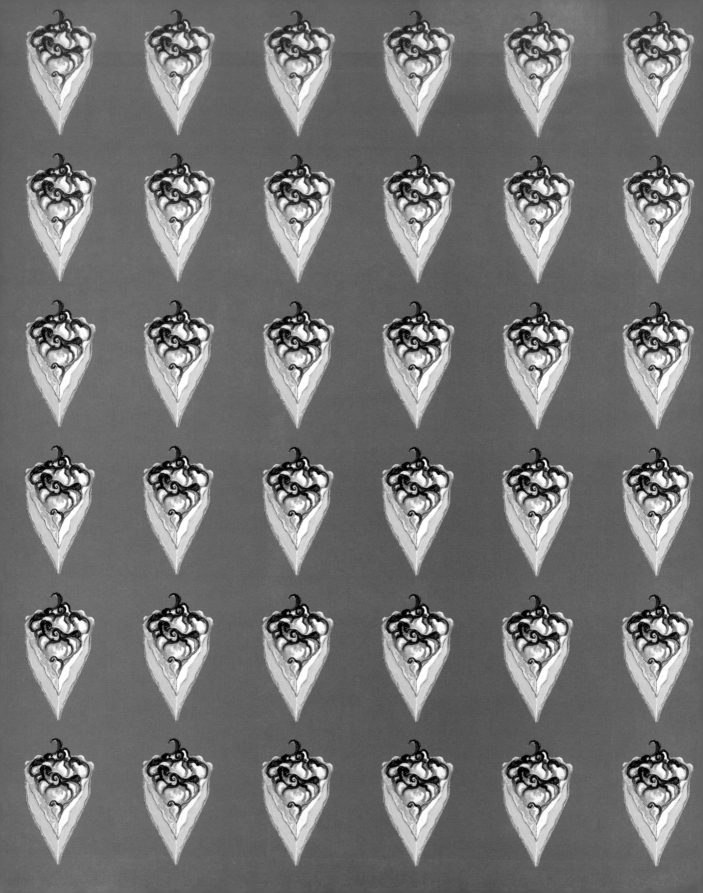

Classics

Classic apple pie

Blueberry pie

Pile high peach pie

Cherry pie

Vanilla cheesecake pie

Lemon meringue pie

Chocolate cloud pie

Key lime pie

Classic tarte tatin

Classic apple pie

The smell of freshly baked apple pie always reminds me of happy trips to visit relatives in America. Crisp buttery pastry with deep layers of apple scented with cinnamon spices and vanilla – there are few more comforting desserts. I use a combination of dessert and cooking apples to balance the sharpness of the fruit, but you can use only cooking apples, if you prefer.

FOR THE PIE CRUST

1 quantity shortcrust pastry (see page 9) or 500 g/18 oz. ready-made shortcrust pastry

1 egg, beaten

FOR THE FILLING

4 cooking apples, peeled and cored

4 dessert apples, peeled and cored

freshly squeezed juice of 1 lemon

2 teaspoons ground cinnamon

60 g/generous ¼ cup soft light brown sugar

115 g/generous ½ cup caster/granulated sugar, plus extra for sprinkling

2 tablespoons plain/all-purpose flour, plus extra for dusting

1 teaspoon pure vanilla extract

a pinch of salt

60 g/½ stick butter, cubed

23-cm/9-in. round pie dish, greased

Serves 6–8

Preheat the oven to 200°C (400°F) Gas 6.

Divide the pastry in half. On a flour-dusted surface, roll out one-half of the pastry into a circle just larger than the size of your pie dish. Using the rolling pin to help lift it, carefully move the pastry into the dish and press it in. Brush the inside of the pastry with some of the beaten egg using a pastry brush. This will help prevent the pastry becoming soggy.

Cut the cooking apples and dessert apples into slices. Place the apples in a bowl and stir in the lemon juice to prevent the apples from going brown. Add the cinnamon, sugars, flour, vanilla extract and salt, and toss together with your hands so everything is well mixed.

Place the apples into the pastry case and dot the top of the fruit with the cubes of butter. Brush the outer edge of the pastry case with a little beaten egg.

Roll out the remaining pastry into a circle just larger than the size of your pie dish and place over the apples. Press together the edges of the pastry base and lid with your fingers. If you want to create a pretty pattern, roll a patterned pastry tool around the edge. Trim away any excess pastry using a knife. You can reroll this out and cut out leaf shapes to decorate the top of your pie, if you wish.

Brush the top of the pie with a little more beaten egg and sprinkle with caster/granulated sugar. Cut a slit in the top of the pie to let any steam escape during cooking.

Bake in the preheated oven for 15 minutes, then reduce the temperature to 170°C (325°F) Gas 3 and bake for about 45 minutes more, until the pie is golden brown and the apples are soft. Remove from the oven and leave to cool for about 15 minutes, then serve immediately with custard or cream. The pie is best eaten on the day it is made, but can be kept for up to 2 days in the refrigerator.

Blueberry pie

This is a classic – rich pastry filled with a purple mound of berries. The aroma of this pie when you remove it from the oven is heavenly, and I find it takes a lot of willpower to resist digging in immediately with a spoon. You can serve it warm with cream or custard, but it is also nice served cold on its own.

FOR THE PIE CRUST

500 g/18 oz. ready-made puff pastry

plain/all-purpose flour, for dusting

1 egg, beaten

FOR THE FILLING

600 g/5 cups blueberries

freshly squeezed juice and grated zest of 2 lemons

100 g/½ cup caster/granulated sugar, plus extra for sprinkling

2 tablespoons cornflour/ cornstarch, sifted

23-cm/9-in. round pie dish, greased

Serves 6-8

Preheat the oven to 200°C (400°F) Gas 6.

On a flour-dusted surface, roll out the pastry thinly using a rolling pin until it is a circle about 6 cm/2½ in. larger than the size of your pie dish. Using the rolling pin to help lift it, carefully move the pastry into the dish and press it down so that it fits snugly in the dish with some of the pastry hanging over the top edge. Brush the inside of the pastry case with some of the beaten egg using a pastry brush. This will help prevent the pastry becoming soggy.

Place the blueberries, lemon juice and zest, sugar and cornflour in a bowl. Stir well so that everything is mixed together.

Spoon the blueberry mixture into the pie dish, piling it high in the centre. Lift the edges of the pastry up over the blueberries and crimp together with your fingers to make a decorative pattern. The centre of the pie should remain open so that you can see the blueberries.

Brush the top of the pastry with the remaining beaten egg and sprinkle with sugar.

Bake the pie in the preheated oven for 40–50 minutes, until the pastry is crisp and golden brown.

Remove from the oven and leave to cool slightly, if serving warm, to allow the sauce to thicken. Alternatively, leave to cool completely and serve cold. This pie is best eaten on the day it is made, although can be stored in an airtight container and eaten the following day if you wish.

Pile high peach pie

Fruit pies should always be bursting with filling and this pie is a perfect example. It is best made in the summer with ripe peaches when they are in season. The pretty heart shapes cut into the crust create an attractive finish.

FOR THE PIE CRUST

1 quantity shortcrust pastry (see page 9) or 500 g/18 oz. ready-made shortcrust pastry

plain/all-purpose flour, for dusting

1 egg, beaten

FOR THE FILLING

8 ripe peaches, stoned/pitted

2 tablespoons cornflour/ cornstarch, sifted

70 g/6 tablespoons caster/ granulated sugar, plus extra for sprinkling

½ teaspoon vanilla salt (or ½ teaspoon salt plus ½ teaspoon vanilla extract)

23-cm/9-in. round pie dish, greased

Serves 6-8

Preheat the oven to 200°C (400°F) Gas 6.

On a flour-dusted surface, roll out one-half of the pastry into a circle just larger than the size of your pie dish. Using the rolling pin to help lift it, carefully move the pastry into the dish and press it down so that it fits snugly. Brush the inside of the pastry with some of the beaten egg using a pastry brush. This will help prevent the pastry becoming soggy.

Cut the peaches into thick slices and place in a bowl with the corn flour/cornstarch, sugar and salt. Toss gently with your hands so that the peaches are coated evenly. Pile the peaches into the pie case.

Roll the remaining pastry out into a circle slightly larger than the size of the dish. Cut out some heart shapes from the centre of the pastry, and reserve the pastry hearts. Brush the edges of the bottom pastry layer with a little beaten egg, then place the second pastry circle on top, so that you can see the filling through the heart-shaped holes. Crimp the edges of the pastry together with your fingertips or with the prongs of a fork, trimming away excess pastry. Brush the top of the pastry with the remaining egg and stick the pastry hearts decoratively on the top, brushing the hearts with a little more beaten egg. Sprinkle with sugar.

Bake in the preheated oven for 30–40 minutes, until the pastry is golden brown. This pie is best eaten on the day it is made, although it can be stored in the refrigerator and eaten the following day if you wish.

Cherry pie

I love cherry pie – this version has a decorative lattice topping and is great to serve in the summer when cherries are ripe and plentiful. If you are short of time, you can replace the filling with a can of cherry pie filling instead, but add the freshly squeezed juice of a lemon to give it a little extra zing.

FOR THE PIE CRUST

500 g/18 oz. ready-made puff pastry

plain/all-purpose flour, for dusting

1 egg, beaten

FOR THE FILLING

400 g/2²/₃ cups cherries, pitted and stalks removed

150 g/³/₄ cup caster/granulated sugar, plus extra for sprinkling

freshly squeezed juice of 1 lemon

15 g/1 tablespoon butter

1 tablespoon cornflour/ cornstarch

23-cm/9-in. round pie dish, greased

Serves 6–8

Begin by preparing the cherry filling, as this needs to cool before making the pie. Simmer the cherries with 80 ml/⅓ cup water, the sugar and the lemon juice in a saucepan, until the cherries are soft and the juice is syrupy. Add the butter and stir until melted. Mix the cornflour with one tablespoon of the cherry juice removed from the pan and then stir into the cherries and juice. Simmer for a few minutes, until the sauce has thickened. Set aside to cool.

Preheat the oven to 200°C (400°F) Gas 6.

On a flour-dusted surface, roll out one-half of the pastry into a circle just larger than the size of your pie dish. Using the rolling pin to help lift it, carefully move the pastry into the dish and press it down so that it fits snugly. Brush the inside of the pastry with some of the beaten egg using a pastry brush, brushing all the way to the edges as the lattice strips need to stick to this edge.

Spoon the cooled cherry filling into the centre of the pastry case. Roll out the remaining pastry into a square just larger than your pie dish, and cut into thin strips. Weave the strips together into a lattice pattern, then transfer the lattice to the pie and press the strips down to join them to the edge of the bottom layer of pastry. Trim any excess pastry with a sharp knife. Brush the top of the pastry with a little more beaten egg and sprinkle with sugar.

Bake in the preheated oven for 25–30 minutes, until the pastry has risen and is golden brown. Serve warm or cold with cream. The pie is best eaten on the day it is made, although can be stored in an airtight container and eaten the following day.

Vanilla cheesecake pie

This delicious cheesecake is encased in a cookie pie crust made with oatmeal and raisin cookies – one of my favourite treats. Serve with fresh raspberries and lashings of cream for extra indulgence.

FOR THE PIE CRUST

450 g/1 lb. chewy oatmeal and raisin cookies

150 g/1¼ sticks butter, melted

FOR THE FILLING

600 ml/2½ cups crème fraîche or sour cream

600 g/2⅔ cups cream cheese

4 eggs

150 g/¾ cup caster/superfine sugar, plus extra for sprinkling

2 tablespoons plain/all-purpose flour, sifted

1 vanilla pod/bean

25-cm/10-in. round, springform cake pan, greased and lined

Serves 12

Preheat the oven to 170°C (325°F) Gas 3.

Blitz the cookies to fine crumbs in a food processor or blender, or place in a clean plastic bag and bash with a rolling pin. Stir in the melted butter then press into the base and sides of the pan firmly, using the back of a spoon. You need the cookie crumbs to come up about 4 cm/1½ in. high on the side of the pan, so that they make a case for the filling. Wrap the outside of the pan in clingfilm/plastic wrap and place in a large roasting pan full of water, so that the water comes about halfway up the pan.

For the filling, whisk together the crème fraîche, cream cheese, eggs, sugar and flour. Using a sharp knife, split the vanilla pod/bean in half, scrape out the seeds from both halves of the pod/bean and add to the cheesecake mixture. (You can store the leftover vanilla pod/bean in a jar of sugar to make vanilla sugar.) Whisk until the seeds are evenly distributed, then pour the mixture into the cookie crust.

Transfer the water bath with the cheesecake in to the oven and bake for 1¼–1½ hours, until the filling is golden brown on top but still has a slight wobble in the centre. Remove the cheesecake from the water and leave to cool, then transfer to the refrigerator to chill for at least 3 hours or, preferably, overnight.

Serve with raspberries and cream if you wish. This pie will keep for up to 3 days stored in the refrigerator.

Lemon meringue pie

With a tangy and vibrant lemon custard and a billowing cloud of meringue topping, lemon meringue pie is a classic dessert. Although it is readily available to buy in supermarkets today, nothing beats a homemade lemon meringue.

FOR THE PIE CRUST

1 quantity shortcrust pastry (see page 9) or 500 g/18 oz. ready-made shortcrust pastry

plain/all-purpose flour, for dusting

FOR THE LEMON FILLING

freshly squeezed juice of 8 lemons and grated zest of 3 lemons

250 g/1¼ cups caster/granulated sugar

80 g/generous ¼ cup cornflour/cornstarch

4 egg yolks (whites reserved for the meringue below)

100 g/7 tablespoons butter

FOR THE MERINGUE

5 egg whites

6 tablespoons caster/granulated sugar

23-cm/9-in. loose-bottom, round, fluted tart pan, greased baking beans

Serves 8

On a flour-dusted surface, roll out the pastry thinly into a circle just larger than the size of your tart pan. Using the rolling pin to help lift it, carefully move the pastry into the pan and press it down so that it fits snugly. Trim away any excess pastry using a sharp knife, but leave some pastry hanging over the edge of the pan. This will be trimmed neatly after the tart is baked. Prick the base with a fork and chill in the refrigerator for 30 minutes.

Preheat the oven to 200°C (400°F) Gas 6.

Line the pastry with baking parchment, fill with baking beans and bake blind in the preheated oven for about 20–25 minutes in the centre of the oven, until the pastry is lightly golden brown (the pastry will cook further while the filling is cooking).

Remove from the oven and, once cool enough to handle, remove the baking beans and parchment. Trim the pastry using a sharp knife so that it is level with the top of the pan. Let cool. Reduce the oven temperature to 180°C (350°F) Gas 4.

For the filling, place the lemon juice, zest and sugar in a saucepan with 500 ml/generous 2 cups water and bring to the boil. Remove from the heat and let cool. Whisk the cornflour/cornstarch with 120 ml/8 tablespoons of the cooled lemon syrup and beat in the eggs. Heat the remaining lemon syrup again and whisk in the cornflour/cornstarch mixture. Stir constantly over the heat, until the mixture thickens. Add the butter to the pan and beat hard. Let cool, then pour into the pastry case. If any lumps have formed in the lemon custard, pass the mixture through a fine sieve/strainer, pressing it through with the back of a spoon.

For the meringue, whisk the egg whites to stiff peaks. Add the sugar, a spoonful at a time, whisking constantly until the meringue is smooth and glossy. Spoon the meringue over the top of the lemon custard and swirl into peaks. Bake in the preheated oven for 25–30 minutes, until the meringue is golden brown and set. Remove from the oven and let cool completely. This pie will keep for up to 3 days stored in the refrigerator.

Chocolate cloud pie

The smell of cocoa when you remove this meringue from the oven is intense and I love to bake this recipe for that reason alone. The delicate chocolate pie shell is filled with a tangy raspberry fool and is topped with curls of chocolate and fresh berries. This is a light but indulgent dessert – perfect for a special occasion.

FOR THE MERINGUE

4 egg whites

250 g/1¼ cups caster/ superfine sugar

½ teaspoon cream of tartar

30 g/scant ⅓ cup unsweetened cocoa powder, sifted

a few cocoa nibs, very finely chopped or ground (optional)

FOR THE RASPBERRY FOOL

300 g/2 cups fresh raspberries

50 g/¼ cup caster/ granulated sugar

500 ml/generous 2 cups double/ heavy cream

TO SERVE

fresh raspberries and chocolate curls

baking sheet, greased and lined with baking parchment

Serves 8

Preheat the oven to 125°C (275°F) Gas 1.

Begin by preparing the meringue. Whisk the egg whites to stiff peaks. Add the sugar, a spoonful at a time, while continuing to whisk. Add the cream of tartar and whisk in. Sift the cocoa over the top of the egg whites and, using a spatula, gently fold in the cocoa. You do not need to fold it in completely as you want there to be a slight rippled effect of cocoa running through the meringue.

Spoon the meringue onto the lined baking sheet and, using the spatula, gently spread it into a 25-cm/10-in. circle, making a well in the centre that will hold the fool. Sprinkle the cocoa nibs over the top of the meringue, if using.

Bake in the preheated oven for about 1½ hours, until the meringue is crisp. Let cool on the baking sheet.

When you are ready to serve, place the meringue on a serving plate. Be careful, as it is very fragile.

Crush the raspberries using a fork, then add the sugar and whisk until the sugar has dissolved and you have a raspberry purée.

In a separate bowl, whisk the cream to stiff peaks, then fold in the raspberry purée in a rippled effect, reserving a little of the raspberry purée for decoration.

Spoon the raspberry fool into the meringue shell very carefully, then drizzle over the reserved raspberry purée. Decorate with more berries and the chocolate curls, and serve immediately. This pie needs to be eaten on the day it is made.

Key lime pie

With hints of chocolate paired with the lime, this dessert reminds me of one of my childhood favourite sweets, chocolate limes. It makes a great dessert as it can be prepared ahead of time. I like to use custard creams/vanilla sandwich cookies for the base, but you can replace them with digestives or graham crackers, if you prefer.

FOR THE PIE CRUST

250 g/9 oz. custard creams/vanilla sandwich cookies or digestive biscuits/graham crackers

100 g/7 tablespoons butter, melted

FOR THE FILLING

6 limes

300 ml/1¼ cups double/heavy cream

400-g/14-oz. can sweetened condensed milk

TO DECORATE

200 ml/scant 1 cup double/heavy cream

chocolate sprinkles

freshly grated lime zest

23-cm/9-in. loose-bottom, round, fluted tart pan, greased

Serves 10

Preheat the oven to 180°C (350°F) Gas 4.

Blitz the cookies to fine crumbs in a food processor or blender, or place in a clean plastic bag and bash with a rolling pin. Stir in the melted butter and then press into the base and the sides of the prepared tart pan firmly using the back of a spoon. Wrap the base and sides of the pan in foil to prevent butter from leaking out, then bake the cookie crust in the oven for 5–8 minutes, then allow to cool completely.

Finely grate the zest of 2 of the limes into a mixing bowl. Add the cream, condensed milk, and the juice of all 6 limes. (Zest the remaining limes before juicing, and reserve for the decoration.) Whisk until smooth. Spoon the mixture into the pie crust and chill in the refrigerator for at least 3 hours, until set, or overnight.

To decorate, place the cream in a bowl and whip to stiff peaks with a whisk. Spoon the whipped cream on top of the pie, and decorate with chocolate sprinkles and the reserved freshly grated lime zest. This pie will keep in the refrigerator for 2 days.

Classic tarte tatin

Tart tatin is one of the most popular desserts — I simply don't know anyone who doesn't like caramelized apples with buttery puff pastry. Serve with Calvados cream or crème fraîche for a perfect dessert with friends. The exact number of apples needed will depend on how large your apples are and the size of your pan.

160 g/generous ¾ cup caster/granulated sugar, plus extra for sprinkling

90 g/¾ stick butter

a pinch of salt

5–7 small dessert apples

freshly squeezed juice of 1 large lemon

500 g/18 oz. ready-made puff pastry

plain/all-purpose flour, for dusting

1 tablespoon full-fat/whole milk

20-cm/8-in. round tatin pan or deep pie dish

Serves 6–8

In a heavy-based saucepan, heat the sugar until it melts and turns golden brown. Do not stir, but swirl the pan to move the sugar to prevent it from burning. Watch closely – as the sugar melts, as it can easily burn. Once caramelized, add the butter and salt to the pan, whisking as it melts. Pour into the base of the tatin pan and let cool.

Preheat the oven to 200°C (400°F) Gas 6.

Peel and core the apples, and cut into quarters. Coat well with the lemon juice to prevent them from discolouring. Place the apples closely together in the pan on top of the caramel.

On a flour-dusted surface, roll the pastry out to about 5 mm/¼ in. thickness and cut out a circle of pastry that is about 1 cm/½ in. larger than your tatin pan. Place the pastry over the apples and tuck it down at the sides of the pan so that the apples are encased. Brush the top of the pastry with milk and sprinkle with a little sugar.

Bake in the preheated oven for 20–30 minutes, until the pastry has risen and is golden brown. Remove from the oven, allow to cool for a few minutes, then carefully invert the pan onto a plate, taking care that you do not burn yourself on the hot caramel. It is best to do this by placing the plate upside-down on top of the pan, then, holding both tightly with oven gloves or a kitchen towel, very quickly turn over, so that the pie ends up apple-side up on your serving plate.

Serve immediately while still warm with cream. This pie is best eaten straight away.

Fresh and fruity

Apricot vanilla tart

Glazed French fruit tart

Pear and amaretto frangipane pie

Glazed mango mousse pie

Baklava banana tarts

Nectarine crumble pie

Tarte au pamplemousse

Pineapple and star anise tarte tatin

Rustic plum tart

Strawberry meringue pies

Cloudberry pie

Rhubarb cloud pie

Blackcurrant cream pie

Apricot vanilla tart

Unless they are really ripe, apricots can taste a little bland, in my view. However, when roasted with a little butter, sugar and lemon juice, they become the perfect topping for this tart. This is a great tart to serve on sunny days when apricots are in abundance.

FOR THE APRICOTS

16 apricots, halved and stones/pits removed

50 g/¼ cup caster/granulated sugar

freshly squeezed juice of 1 lemon

50 g/3½ tablespoons butter

FOR THE PIE CRUST

1 quantity shortcrust pastry (see page 9) or 500 g/18 oz. ready-made shortcrust pastry

plain/all-purpose flour, for dusting

FOR THE FILLING

250 g/generous 1 cup mascarpone cheese

150 ml/⅔ cup crème fraîche

100 g/3½ oz. vanilla custard

½ teaspoon vanilla bean powder or 1 teaspoon vanilla extract

1 heaped tablespoon icing/confectioners' sugar, sifted

FOR THE GLAZE

2 tablespoons apricot glaze or apricot jam/jelly

freshly squeezed juice of 1 lemon

23-cm/9-in. loose-bottom, round, fluted tart pan, greased

baking beans

Serves 8

Preheat the oven to 180°C (350°F) Gas 4.

Place the apricots, cut-side down, in a roasting pan and sprinkle with the sugar and lemon juice. Add the butter and bake for 15–20 minutes, until the fruit is just soft. Remove from the oven and let cool. Increase the oven temperature to 200°C (400°F) Gas 6.

On a flour-dusted surface, roll out the pastry thinly into a circle just larger than the size of your tart pan. Using the rolling pin to help lift it, carefully move the pastry into the pan and press it down so that it fits snugly. Trim away any excess pastry using a sharp knife, but leave some pastry hanging over the edge of the pan. This will be trimmed neatly after the tart is baked. Prick the base with a fork and chill in the refrigerator for 30 minutes.

Line the pastry case with baking parchment, fill with baking beans and bake blind for about 20–25 minutes in the centre of the preheated oven, until the pastry is golden brown and crisp. When cool enough to handle, remove the baking beans and parchment. Trim the edge of the pastry with a sharp knife by running it along the top of the pan.

Blitz about one-third of the apricots and the cooking syrup to a purée in a food processor or blender and pass through a fine-mesh sieve/strainer so that the purée is smooth. In a bowl, whisk together the apricot purée, mascarpone cheese, crème fraîche, custard, vanilla and icing/confectioners' sugar until smooth. Spoon the mixture into the pie crust and spread out evenly using a spatula.

Place the remaining apricots on top of the cream filling, moving them carefully with a spatula so that they retain their shape.

In a saucepan, heat the apricot glaze and lemon juice until melted. If using apricot jam, you may need to strain the heated syrup to remove any apricot pieces. Leave to cool slightly, then brush over the top of the fruit with a pastry brush.

Chill in the refrigerator for at least 2 hours before serving. This pie will keep for up to 3 days stored in the refrigerator.

Glazed French fruit tart

When on holiday in France, I love gazing in the windows of patisseries, looking at the delicious gâteaux and tarts on display. My favourites are always the glazed fruit tarts. You can decorate this tart with any fruit of your choosing – my choice is usually red and black summer berries – even wild strawberries, if you are lucky enough to find them.

FOR THE PIE CRUST

115 g/1 stick butter, chilled

280 g/generous 2 cups plain/all-purpose flour, sifted, plus extra for dusting

a pinch of salt

grated zest of 1 orange

FOR THE FILLING

100 g/3½ oz. plain/semisweet chocolate, melted

250 g/generous 1 cup mascarpone cheese

300 ml/1¼ cups crème fraîche

2 heaped tablespoons icing/confectioners' sugar, sifted

½ teaspoon vanilla bean powder or 1 teaspoon pure vanilla extract

TO DECORATE

fresh berries of your choosing

1 packet glaze topping/fixing gel, such as Dr Oetker's (or 3 tablespoons apricot glaze)

1 teaspoon pure vanilla extract

1 tablespoon Grand Marnier or orange liqueur

23-cm/9-in. loose-bottom, fluted tart pan, greased

baking beans

Serves 8–10

For the pastry, rub the butter into the flour and salt using your fingertips. Add the orange zest and 1 tablespoon of cold water, and mix in with a round-bladed knife, adding a little more water if the mixture is too dry. Wrap the pastry in clingfilm/plastic wrap and chill in the refrigerator for 30 minutes.

On a flour-dusted surface, roll out the pastry thinly into a circle just larger than the size of your tart pan. Using the rolling pin to help lift it, carefully move the pastry into the pan and press it down so that it fits snugly. Trim away any excess pastry using a sharp knife, but leave some pastry hanging over the edge of the pan. This will be trimmed neatly after the tart is baked. Prick the base with a fork and chill in the refrigerator for 30 minutes.

Preheat the oven to 200°C (400°F) Gas 6.

Line the pastry with baking parchment and fill with baking beans. Bake the pastry for 20–25 minutes, until lightly golden brown and crisp, then remove from the oven and let cool. When cool enough to handle, remove the baking beans and parchment. Trim the edge of the pastry by running a sharp knife along the edge of the pan.

Spread the melted chocolate over the base of the cooled pastry case.

For the filling, whisk together the mascarpone, crème fraîche, icing/confectioners' sugar and vanilla until smooth and creamy. Spoon into the pie crust and spread out evenly. Decorate the top of the tart with fresh berries, arranging them so that all of the cream is covered.

To glaze, prepare the glaze topping/fixing gel according to the packet instructions, adding the vanilla extract and Grand Marnier to the mixture with the water. Leave until just cool, then spoon over the fruit. If you are using apricot glaze instead, heat it in a saucepan with the Grand Marnier and vanilla, let cool slightly and then brush in a thick layer over the tart to glaze using a pastry brush.

Allow to cool before serving. This pie can be kept for up to 2 days in the refrigerator, but is best eaten on the day it is made.

Pear and amaretto frangipane pie

This dessert is inspired by a cocktail I drank on holiday in Portugal – Amendoa Amarga (a Portuguese almond liqueur) served with lemon juice over ice. This versatile pie is equally at home served for afternoon tea as it is for an elegant dessert with a spoonful of whipped or clotted cream.

FOR THE POACHED PEARS

4 ripe pears

2 tablespoons runny honey

80 ml/⅓ cup amaretto liqueur

freshly squeezed juice of 2 lemons

FOR THE PIE CRUST

1 quantity shortcrust pastry (see page 9) or 500 g/18 oz. ready-made shortcrust pastry

plain/all-purpose flour, for dusting

FOR THE FRANGIPANE

120 g/scant ⅔ cup caster/ granulated sugar

125 g/9 tablespoons butter, softened

3 UK large/US extra-large eggs

grated zest of 1 lemon

60 ml/4 tablespoons amaretto liqueur

200 g/2 cups ground almonds

FOR THE GLAZE

1 tablespoon orange marmalade

freshly squeezed juice of 1 lemon

1 tablespoon caster/ granulated sugar

23-cm/9-in. loose-bottom, round, fluted tart pan, greased

Serves 8–10

Begin by poaching the pears, as they need to cool before being used in the pie. Peel the pears, leaving the stalks intact. Place them in a large saucepan with the honey, amaretto and lemon juice and enough water to cover them. Simmer over a gentle heat for 20–30 minutes, until the pears are just soft. Let cool in the poaching liquid, then remove and drain well. Cut each pear in half, removing the core and stalk using a teaspoon. Using a sharp knife, score thin lines in the rounded sides of each pear half, taking care not to cut all the way through.

On a flour-dusted surface, roll out the pastry thinly into a circle just larger than the size of your tart pan. Using the rolling pin to help lift it, carefully move the pastry into the pan and press it down so that it fits snugly. Trim away any excess pastry using a sharp knife, but leave some pastry hanging over the edge of the pan. This will be trimmed neatly after the tart is baked. Prick the base with a fork and chill in the refrigerator for 30 minutes.

Preheat the oven to 180°C (350°F) Gas 4.

For the frangipane, cream together the sugar and butter in a mixing bowl. Add the eggs and whisk in with the lemon zest and amaretto liqueur. Finally, whisk in the ground almonds so that you have a smooth paste. Spoon the paste into the chilled pie crust, and then place the pears at even intervals around the pie, cut-side up, pressing them into the frangipane.

Bake the pie in the preheated oven for 30–40 minutes, until the frangipane and pastry are golden brown. Remove from the oven. Trim the edge of the pastry with a sharp knife by running it along the top of the pan.

In a saucepan, heat the marmalade, lemon juice and sugar. Pass through a sieve/strainer to remove any peel and then brush over the top of the pie using a pastry brush. Serve the pie warm or cold with whipped cream. This pie will keep for up to 2 days stored in an airtight container.

Glazed mango mousse pie

Tropical mangoes are juicy and tangy, and they make the perfect filling for this sunshine pie. Topped with thin slices of mango and strawberries, this pie looks as pretty as a picture. Make your own glaze or use a store-bought one to save time.

FOR THE PIE CRUST
250 g/9 oz. ginger biscuits/cookies

150 g/1¼ sticks butter, melted

FOR THE MANGO MOUSSE
1 large ripe mango

70 g/5⅔ tablespoons caster/superfine sugar

freshly squeezed juice of 1 lemon

12 g/4 teaspoons powdered gelatine

300 ml/1¼ cups double/heavy cream

TO DECORATE
1 ripe mango

about 20 fresh strawberries

FOR THE GLAZE
2 sheets of leaf gelatine

freshly squeezed juice of 2 lemons

30 g/2½ tablespoons caster/superfine sugar

1 packet glaze topping/fixing gel, such as Dr Oetker's (optional)

35 x 10-cm/14 x 4-in. loose-bottom, rectangular, fluted tart pan, greased

Serves 8

Blitz the biscuits/cookies to fine crumbs in a food processor or blender, or place in a clean plastic bag and bash with a rolling pin. Add the melted butter and sugar, and mix again so that all the crumbs are coated in butter. Using the back of a spoon, press the crumb mixture into the prepared pan so that the sides have a thick layer of crumbs on and the base is completely covered, with no gaps.

For the mousse, peel the mango and chop the flesh away from the stone/pit. Place the flesh in a blender with the sugar and lemon juice, and blitz to a smooth purée. Dissolve the gelatine in 1 tablespoon of warm water and then add to the mango mixture. Whip the cream to stiff peaks and then fold through the mango purée, whisking gently so that it is all incorporated. Pour the mousse into the pie crust and chill in the refrigerator for at least 3 hours.

When the mousse is set, finely slice the mango and strawberries for decoration, and arrange in patterns on top of the mango mousse.

If you are making your own glaze, soak the gelatine leaves in cold water. Heat the lemon juice with 250 ml/generous 1 cup of water and the sugar, until the sugar has dissolved and the mixture is warm but not boiling (having the liquid too hot will affect the setting properties of the gelatine). Stir in the gelatine until dissolved, then strain through a sieve/strainer. Leave until just cool. Alternatively, prepare the glaze topping/fixing gel according to the packet instructions. Pour the glaze over the fruit and leave to set in the fridge overnight.

This pie will keep for up to 2 days in the refrigerator.

Baklava banana tarts

Baklava is a popular Greek dessert – crispy, buttery pastry filled with nuts and soaked in honey – utterly delicious. These little baklava tarts contain banana purée, which adds a fruity dimension.

FOR THE FILLINGS

100 g/scant ¾ cup walnuts

1 teaspoon ground cinnamon

40 g/3¼ tablespoons Demerara/raw sugar

2 ripe bananas

freshly squeezed juice of 1 lemon

TO ASSEMBLE

250 g/9 oz. filo/phyllo pastry

125 g/9 tablespoons butter, melted

3 tablespoons honey

3 tablespoons maple syrup

12-hole muffin pan, greased

8-cm/3¼-in. round cutter

Makes 12

Begin by preparing the fillings. Place the walnuts, cinnamon and Demerara/raw sugar in a food processor or blender and blitz to fine crumbs. In a separate bowl, crush the bananas with the lemon juice using the back of a fork to make a banana purée.

Preheat the oven to 180°C (350°F) Gas 4.

You will need to cut out 24 squares of pastry, 11 x 11 cm/4¼ x 4¼ in., and approximately 72 circles, 8 cm/3¼ in. diameter. The filo/phyllo pastry dries out quickly, so it is best to cover it with a clean damp kitchen towel while you are assembling the tarts, and only cut the pastry as and when you need it.

Brush the squares of pastry with melted butter and place two into one of the holes of the muffin pan at slight angles to each other. Sprinkle a small spoonful of the nut mixture into the base of each pastry case. Cover the nuts with two circles of pastry, both brushed with butter. Place a spoonful of banana purée on top of the pastry, and then cover with two further buttered circles of pastry. Sprinkle with more nuts and finish the pie with two further layers of pastry. Continue to make more layers, until the muffin hole is full and finished with a filo/phyllo layer on top. How many sheets you need will depend on how deep your muffin pan is. Repeat to make the remaining tarts.

Bake in the preheated oven for 25–30 minutes, until the pastry is golden brown. Heat the honey and maple syrup in a saucepan and pour a little over the top of each pie. The pies can be eaten warm or cold, and are best eaten on the day they are made.

Nectarine crumble pie

In the summer months, when nectarines are ripe and juicy, this pie is a real treat, bursting with fruit and topped with an almond crumble. This recipe is for Harry Weatherstone, who is only young but is an amazing cook.

FOR THE PIE CRUST

1 quantity shortcrust pastry (see page 9) or 500 g/18 oz. ready-made shortcrust pastry

plain/all-purpose flour, for dusting

1 egg, beaten

FOR THE FILLING

6 ripe nectarines

100 g/½ cup caster/granulated sugar

2 tablespoons cornflour/cornstarch

½ teaspoon salt

1 teaspoon vanilla bean powder or pure vanilla extract

FOR THE CRUMBLE TOPPING

150 g/5½ oz. amaretti biscuits/cookies

130 g/4½ oz. golden marzipan

100 g/7 tablespoons butter, melted

icing/confectioners' sugar, for dusting

23-cm/9-in. round pie dish, greased

Serves 8–10

On a flour-dusted surface, roll out the pastry thinly into a circle just larger than the size of your tart pan. Using the rolling pin to help lift it, carefully move the pastry into the pan and press it down so that it fits snugly. Trim away any excess pastry using a sharp knife. Use the trimmings to create a decorative border and stick it to the edge using a little beaten egg. Prick the base with a fork and chill in the refrigerator for 30 minutes.

Preheat the oven to 180°C (350°F) Gas 4.

To prepare the crumble topping, crush the amaretti biscuits/cookies into small pieces with your hands. Chop the marzipan into small pieces and add to the crushed amaretti biscuits/cookies. Stir in the warm melted butter and squash the mixture together with your hands so that everything is mixed well and you have a crumble mixture.

For the filling, remove the stones/pits from the nectarines and cut the flesh into large chunks. Place in a mixing bowl with the sugar, cornflour/cornstarch, salt and vanilla powder. Stir together gently. Brush the bottom of the pastry crust with a thin layer of beaten egg using a pastry brush and then place the nectarines on top. Sprinkle over the crumble topping.

Bake in the preheated oven for 30–40 minutes, until the pastry is golden brown. If the crumble topping starts to turn dark, cover loosely with foil. Serve warm or cold, dusted with icing/confectioners' sugar. This pie will keep for up to 2 days stored in the refrigerator.

Tarte au pamplemousse

You are going to have to trust me on this one. This was a recipe that I first made as an experiment – with some trepidation, as grapefruit and cream are not a natural pairing. But I love the flavour of grapefruit and wanted to see it if was possible to use it as an alternative to a classic lemon tart. It was a resounding success and the tart was devoured by my friends at work in less than an hour!

FOR THE PIE CRUST

1 quantity shortcrust pastry (see page 9) or 500 g/18 oz. ready-made shortcrust pastry

plain/all-purpose flour, for dusting

1 egg, beaten

FOR THE CUSTARD

9 eggs

350 g/1¾ cups caster/ granulated sugar, plus extra for sprinkling

freshly squeezed juice of 2 ruby red grapefruit

1 tablespoon mint leaves

1 tablespoon lemon and mint cordial

300 ml/1¼ cups double/ heavy cream

23-cm/9-in. loose-bottom, round, fluted tart pan, greased

baking beans

chef's blow torch

Serves 10

On a flour-dusted surface, roll out the pastry thinly into a circle just larger than the size of your tart pan. Using the rolling pin to help lift it, carefully move the pastry into the pan and press it down so that it fits snugly. Trim away any excess pastry using a sharp knife, but leave some pastry hanging over the edge of the pan. This will be trimmed neatly after the tart is baked. Prick the base with a fork and chill in the refrigerator for 30 minutes.

Preheat the oven to 200°C (400°F) Gas 6.

Line the pastry with baking parchment, fill with baking beans and bake blind for about 15–20 minutes in the centre of the preheated oven, until the pastry is golden brown. Turn the temperature down to 180°C (350°F) Gas 4. Once cool enough to handle, remove the beans and parchment. Use a sharp knife to slice away the excess pastry around the top of the pan, so that the pastry is in line with the top of the pan.

Whisk together the eggs, sugar, grapefruit juice (sieved/strained to remove any pips), mint and cordial together in a bowl. Slowly pour in the cream, whisking all the time. Place in a heatproof bowl and set over a pan of simmering water until the mixture becomes just warm. This will take about 5 minutes. Strain the mixture to remove the mint, then pour into the pastry crust. You may not need all of the filling, depending on the size of your pan. Bake for 30–40 minutes, until the top of the custard is lightly golden and has risen. Remove from the oven and let cool. The custard will sink back into the tart case as it cools.

Just before serving, sprinkle the top of the pie with a thin layer of caster/granulated sugar, and then caramelize into a brûlée topping using a chef's blow torch, taking care that the sugar does not burn. Serve immediately, as the sugar topping will become less crisp over time.

Pineapple and star anise tarte tatin

While tarte tatins are traditionally made with apples, pineapple also works brilliantly. It releases its golden juices into the caramel on cooking, which gives it a distinctly tropical flavour. The star anise, although not edible, imparts a delicate hint of aniseed into the caramel as well.

140 g/scant ¾ cup caster/
granulated sugar, plus extra
for sprinkling

80 g/¾ stick butter

a pinch of salt

1 ripe pineapple

8 star anise

500 g/18 oz. ready-made
puff pastry

plain/all-purpose flour,
for dusting

milk, for brushing

*two 4-hole Yorkshire pudding
pans (with 10-cm/4-in. holes),
greased, or 10-cm/4-in. mini tatin
pans, greased*

10-cm/4-in. round cookie cutter

Makes 8

In a heavy-based saucepan, heat the sugar until it melts and turns golden brown. Do not stir, but swirl the pan to prevent the sugar from burning. Watch closely as the sugar melts, as it can easily burn. Once caramelized, add the butter and salt to the pan, whisking as it melts to make a caramel sauce. Divide the caramel equally between the holes of the Yorkshire pudding pans or mini tatin pans and leave to cool.

Peel and core the pineapple and cut into 8 rings. (If you are short of time you can use tinned/canned pineapple instead.) Place a ring of pineapple into each hole and press a star anise into the centre of each pineapple ring.

Preheat the oven to 200°C (400°F) Gas 6.

On a flour-dusted surface, roll the pastry thinly and cut out 8 discs of pastry using a 10-cm/4-in. round cutter. If you do not have a large enough cutter, use a small plate or bowl as a template to cut round, using a sharp knife.

Press the pastry tightly over the pineapple, crimping around the edges. Brush the pastry with a little milk to glaze and sprinkle with a little sugar.

Bake in the preheated oven for 15–20 minutes, until the pastry has risen and is golden brown. Remove from the oven, allow to cool for a few minutes, then carefully invert the pans onto a tray, taking care that you do not burn yourself on the hot caramel. Serve immediately, with whipped cream flavoured with coconut rum if you wish. The star anise are for flavouring purposes only and should not be eaten. These tarts are best eaten on the day they are made.

Rustic plum tart

I have a large plum tree in my garden which produces a glut of fruit in early summer. There is nothing I like more than making plum pie with my own plums. You can use a few different varieties of plums to create a decorative coloured pattern, if you wish.

FOR THE PIE CRUST

500 g/18 oz. ready-made puff pastry

plain/all-purpose flour, for dusting

1 egg, beaten

FOR THE FILLING

100 g/3½ oz. golden marzipan

100 g/1 cup ground almonds

50 g/¼ cup caster/granulated sugar, plus extra to sprinkle

about 16–18 plums

FOR THE GLAZE

2 tablespoons apricot glaze or apricot jam

20-cm/8-in. square, loose-bottom, fluted tart pan, greased

Serves 6–8

Preheat the oven to 200°C (400°F) Gas 6.

On a flour-dusted surface, roll out the pastry thinly into a square using a rolling pin until it is about 6 cm/2¼ in. larger than the size of your pan. Using the rolling pin to help lift, carefully move the pastry into the pan and press it down so that it fits tightly into the corners of the pan. Brush the inside of the pastry case with some of the beaten egg using a pastry brush. This will help prevent the pastry becoming soggy. Grate the marzipan coarsely on a grater and then lightly stir in the ground almonds and sugar. Sprinkle the almond mixture into the pastry case in an even layer.

Cut the plums in quarters and remove the stones. Place the plum quarters in rows in the pan in a decorative pattern. Pull the pastry edges up around the side of the plums. Brush the pastry with the remaining egg and sprinkle the fruit and pastry with a little extra sugar.

Bake the pie in the preheated oven for 30–40 minutes, until the pastry has puffed up and is golden brown and the fruit still holds its shape but has released some of its juices. Remove from the oven.

Heat the apricot glaze or jam in a saucepan and then brush over the warm plums to glaze. Serve immediately if you want to eat warm, but this tart is also nice served cold with whipped cream. It will keep for up to 2 days in an airtight container.

Strawberry meringue pies

Strawberries and meringue are, to me, the perfect dessert to serve on a hot summer's day. This pie contains a tangy strawberry mousse filling, a layer of fresh berries and an indulgent toasted Italian meringue topping that is reminiscent of marshmallows toasted on a barbecue.

FOR THE PIE CRUST
250 g/9 oz. lemon shortbread or lemon-flavoured biscuits/cookies
150 g/1¼ sticks butter, melted

FOR THE STRAWBERRY MOUSSE
200 g/2 cups strawberries
100 g/½ cup caster/granulated sugar
½ teaspoon vanilla bean powder or 1 teaspoon pure vanilla extract
12 g/4 teaspoons powdered gelatine
300 ml/1¼ cups double/heavy cream

FOR THE STRAWBERRY MERINGUE LAYER
150 g/¾ cup caster/granulated sugar
60 ml/4 tablespoons golden syrup/light corn syrup
3 egg whites
250 g/2½ cups strawberries, hulled and chopped

four 8-cm/3-in. loose-bottom, deep, round cake pans, greased
chef's blow torch
piping/pastry bag fitted with a large round nozzle/tip

Makes 4

Blitz the shortbread to fine crumbs in a food processor or blender, or place in a clean plastic bag and bash with a rolling pin. Add the melted butter and mix again, so that all the crumbs are coated in butter. Using the back of a spoon, press the cookie crumb mixture into the prepared pans, so that the sides have a thick layer of crumbs on and the bases are completely covered, with no gaps. Chill in the refrigerator for 30 minutes.

For the mousse, place the strawberries in a saucepan with the sugar, vanilla bean powder and 100 ml/generous ⅓ cup water and simmer until the fruit is soft. Pass the mixture through a sieve/strainer, pressing down the strawberries with the back of a spoon to pass them through the sieve/strainer. Discard any pieces that will not pass through. Return the strawberry syrup to the pan and heat gently, then sprinkle the gelatine over the surface of the liquid and whisk in. Do not boil the liquid as this can cause the gelatine to lose its setting properties. Leave until just cool.

Place the cooled strawberry syrup and cream in a bowl and whip to soft peaks. The mixture will not form stiff peaks given the liquid quantity but will set firm in the refrigerator due to the gelatine, so do not worry if it seems runny. Divide the mousse between the pie crusts and chill in the refrigerator for at least 3 hours.

To make the meringue, heat the sugar, syrup and 4 tablespoons of water in a saucepan until the sugar has dissolved, then bring to the boil. Whisk the egg whites to stiff peaks. Gradually pour the hot sugar syrup into the egg whites in a thin stream and whisk until the meringue cools down. This will take about 10 minutes and is therefore best done with a stand mixer. Spoon the meringue into a piping/pastry bag.

Remove the pies from the refrigerator and top the mousse with the chopped strawberries. Pipe the meringue onto the pies in high peaks or swirls. Lightly brown the meringue with a chef's blow torch or under a hot grill/broiler. Serve immediately. These pies are best eaten on the day they are made.

Cloudberry pie

The cloudberry is a Scandinavian yellow berry which is similar to a raspberry. It tastes absolutely delicious. The only sadness is that I have yet to find the fresh berries outside Scandinavia. The next best thing is cloudberry jam, which is available in the UK and US online and in Scandinavian food stores. If you see a jar, buy it and treat yourself to this delicious pie!

FOR THE PIE CRUST

300 g/10½ oz. chocolate sandwich cookies, such as Oreos

125 g/9 tablespoons butter

FOR THE FILLING

4 sheets platinum-grade gelatine

200 g/scant 1 cup cream cheese

250 g/generous 1 cup mascarpone cheese

250 ml/generous 1 cup double/heavy cream

280 g/1 cup cloudberry jam/jelly

freshly squeezed juice of 1 lemon

FOR THE MERINGUE

2 egg whites

100 g/½ cup caster/granulated sugar

1 tablespoon golden syrup/light corn syrup

25-cm/10-in. springform, round pan, greased and lined

chef's blow torch

Serves 10

Crush the cookies to fine crumbs in a food processor or blender, or place in a clean plastic bag and bash with a rolling pin. Stir in the melted butter then press into the base and sides of the pan firmly using the back of a spoon. You need the biscuit crumbs to come up about 4 cm/1½ in. high on the side of the pan so that they make a case for the filling.

For the cloudberry mousse, soak the gelatine leaves in cold water until soft. Whisk together the cream cheese, mascarpone, cream and 3 large spoonfuls of the cloudberry jam. Heat the lemon juice and 4 tablespoons of water until just warm. Squeeze the water out from the gelatine leaves and add the gelatine leaves to the warm lemon juice. Stir until the gelatine has dissolved, then strain through a sieve/strainer and add to the cream mixture. Whisk together and pour into the pie crust. Leave to set in the refrigerator for at least 3 hours.

Spread the remaining jam/jelly over the set mousse. For the meringue, whisk the egg whites to stiff peaks. Heat the sugar and corn syrup with 3 tablespoons of water until the sugar has dissolved. Bring to the boil then pour into the egg whites in a thin stream, whisking all the time. Spoon the meringue over the top of the pie and use a fork to spread it out evenly and create lines on the top. Toast the meringue with a chef's blow torch until lightly caramelized. Carefully slide a knife around the side of the pie crust and remove the pie from the pan. Place on a serving plate to serve. This pie will keep for up to 2 days in the refrigerator, but it is best eaten on the day it is made.

Rhubarb cloud pie

There are many steps to this pie, but it is definitely worth trying. With creamy custard, sweet meringue, buttery base and tangy rhubarb, this is a decadent dessert.

FOR THE RHUBARB TUILES
3 sticks rhubarb
a few drops pink food colouring
freshly squeezed juice of 1 lemon
1 tablespoon caster/
granulated sugar

FOR THE BASE
200 g/7 oz. custard creams/
vanilla sandwich cookies
100 g/7 tablespoons butter,
melted

FOR THE MERINGUE SHELL
4 egg whites
½ teaspoon cream of tartar
250 g/1¼ cups caster/
granulated sugar

FOR THE CUSTARD
4 egg yolks
50 g/¼ cup caster/
granulated sugar
½ teaspoon vanilla bean powder
or 1 teaspoon pure vanilla extract
250 ml/generous 1 cup double/
heavy cream

FOR THE TOPPING
400 g/14 oz. rhubarb
1 tablespoon caster/
granulated sugar
300 ml/1¼ cup double/
heavy cream, whipped

silicone mat
23-cm/9-in. round, springform
cake pan, greased and lined

Serves 8

Begin by preparing the rhubarb tuiles, as they need to dry overnight. Trim the ends of the rhubarb and peel into long thin strips using a swivel peeler. Place the strips of rhubarb in a large saucepan with just enough water to cover and add the food colouring, lemon juice and sugar. Simmer for 2–3 minutes, until just soft. Put the rhubarb onto a silicone mat and twist into pretty shapes. Leave in a warm place to dry overnight, until the rhubarb is crisp. Store carefully in an airtight container.

Preheat the oven to 180°C (350°F) Gas 4.

To make the topping, peel and chop the rhubarb into 5-cm/2-in. lengths. Place in an ovenproof dish, add the sugar and 2 tablespoons water, and toss together to coat. Bake for 20–25 minutes, until the rhubarb is soft but still holding its shape. Drain away any liquid and set aside to cool. Reduce the oven temperature to 140°C (275°F) Gas 1.

For the base, blitz the cookies to fine crumbs in a food processor or place in a clean plastic bag and bash with a rolling pin. Add the melted butter and blitz again so that all the crumbs are coated. Using the back of a spoon, press the crumb mixture into the base of the prepared pan. Wrap the bottom and sides of the pan in foil to stop the butter leaking out.

For the meringue shell, whisk the egg whites to stiff peaks. Sprinkle over the cream of tartar and, while whisking, add the sugar, a spoonful at a time, until you have a smooth glossy meringue. Spoon the meringue onto the cookie crumb base and, using a spatula, spread it across the base and up the sides to form a case to hold the custard filling.

For the custard, whisk the egg yolks and sugar until thick and creamy. Heat the vanilla and cream in a saucepan and bring to the boil. Remove from the heat and pour over the egg mixture, whisking all the time. Return the custard to the saucepan and cook over a gentle heat, whisking constantly, until it starts to thicken. If the mixture starts to curdle, pass it through a sieve/strainer. Transfer to a bowl and let cool for a few minutes.

Pour the custard into the meringue shell and bake for 1½-2 hours, until the meringue is crisp and the custard is set but still wobbly in the centre. Slide a knife around the sides of the pan and let cool in the pan.

Remove the sides of the pan and place the pie on a serving plate, removing the lining paper. Place the cooled baked rhubarb on top of the custard. Spoon over the whipped cream and top with the rhubarb tuiles. Serve immediately. Any uneaten pie can be stored in the refrigerator for up to 2 days, but this pie is best eaten on the day it is made.

Blackcurrant cream pie

My Welsh grandpa used to grow blackcurrants in his garden, and when I was little, I would spend afternoons picking them with him, and we would then make them into pies and tarts. He was an excellent baker. This pie is in memory of him – filled with a creamy lemon custard and topped with blackcurrants.

FOR THE PIE CRUST

1 quantity shortcrust pastry (see page 9) or 500 g/18 oz. ready-made shortcrust pastry

plain/all-purpose flour, for dusting

FOR THE FILLING

6 egg yolks

70 g/5⅓ tablespoons caster/granulated sugar

400 ml/1¾ cups double/heavy cream

1 teaspoon vanilla bean powder

grated zest of 1 lemon

900 g/2 lb. blackcurrants in light syrup (345 g/¾ lb. drained weight), syrup reserved

FOR THE GLAZE

2 sheets of leaf gelatine

freshly squeezed juice of 2 lemons

30 g/2½ tablespoons caster/granulated sugar

1 packet glaze topping/fixing gel, such as Dr Oetker's (optional)

23-cm/9-in. loose-bottom, round, fluted tart pan, greased

baking beans

Serves 10

On a flour-dusted surface, roll out the pastry thinly into a circle just larger than the size of your tart pan. Using the rolling pin to help lift it, carefully move the pastry into the pan and press it down so that it fits snugly. Trim away any excess pastry using a sharp knife, but leave some pastry hanging over the edge of the pan. This will be trimmed neatly after the tart is baked. Prick the base with a fork and chill in the refrigerator for 30 minutes.

Preheat the oven to 180°C (350°F) Gas 4.

Line the pastry with baking parchment, fill with baking beans and bake blind for about 15–20 minutes, until the pastry is golden brown. When cool enough to handle, remove the beans and parchment. Trim the edge of the pastry to the level of the pan using a sharp knife. Reduce the oven temperature to 150°C (300°F) Gas 2.

Whisk together the egg yolks and sugar until light and creamy. Slowly pour in the cream, vanilla and lemon zest, and whisk everything together. Drain the blackcurrants and reserve the syrup. Stir one-third of the blackcurrants into the custard gently. Pour into a jug/pitcher and then slowly pour into the pie crust. Transfer carefully to the oven.

Bake for about 1½ hours, until the top of the tart is very lightly golden brown and set with a slight wobble. Let cool. Cover the top of the tart with the remaining blackcurrants.

If you are making your own glaze, soak the gelatine leaves in cold water. Heat the lemon juice with the sugar and 250 ml/generous 1 cup of the light blackcurrant syrup drained from the fruit, until the sugar has dissolved and the mixture is warm but not boiling (having the liquid too hot will affect the setting properties of the gelatine). Stir in the gelatine, until dissolved, then strain through a sieve/strainer. Leave until just cool. Alternatively, prepare the glaze topping/fixing gel according to packet instructions, using the light blackcurrant syrup drained from the fruit in place of the water specified, then pour over the fruit and leave to set in the refrigerator overnight. This pie will keep for up to 3 days stored in the refrigerator.

Rich and indulgent

Chocolate fondant mini tarts

Mocha chocolate almond pie

Salted caramel pie

Coffee cream pie

Walnut custard tart

Prune and Armagnac tarts

Glazed cinnamon nut pie

Chocolate pistachio pie

Malted mascarpone pie

Raspberry and rose tartlets

Hazelnut croquant pie

Chocolate fondant mini tarts

When I was on MasterChef, chocolate fondants were notorious for going wrong, as they often failed to have the gooey, runny centre. The secret is not to cook them for too long. I have used that delicious molten cake mixture to fill these chocolate-cookie-crust tart cases for a rich and indulgent dessert. Serve with fresh berries and crème fraîche to cut through the richness of the tarts, if you like.

FOR THE PIE CRUST

250 g/9 oz. digestive biscuits/
graham crackers

30 g/⅓ cup unsweetened
cocoa powder, plus extra
for dusting

115 g/1 stick butter, melted

FOR THE FILLING

40 g/3 tablespoons butter,
softened

60 g/5 tablespoons soft dark
brown sugar

60 g/5 tablespoons caster/
granulated sugar

3 eggs

a pinch of vanilla salt
(or regular salt)

40 g/5 tablespoons plain/
all-purpose flour

250 g/9 oz. dark/bittersweet
chocolate (70% cocoa solids),
melted and cooled

four 12-cm/5-in. loose-bottom,
round, fluted tart pans, greased

Serves 4

For the pie crust, blitz the biscuits/crackers to fine crumbs in a food processor or place in a clean plastic bag and bash with a rolling pin. Stir in the cocoa powder and melted butter, ensuring that all the crumbs are well coated. Press the crumbs into the base and sides of the pans firmly, using the back of a spoon.

Preheat the oven to 200°C (400°F) Gas 6.

For the filling, whisk together the butter and both sugars until creamy. Add the eggs, salt and flour, and whisk again. Fold in the melted chocolate. Wrap the base and sides of the pans in foil to prevent butter leaking out, then divide the chocolate mixture between the pans and bake in the preheated oven for 10–12 minutes, until the tops are set but the filling is still soft in the middle.

The tarts can be served immediately and eaten warm or left to cool, as they are equally delicious either way. They are best eaten on the day they are made, but can be stored for up to 2 days in an airtight container.

To serve, dust with a little cocoa powder.

Mocha chocolate almond pie

This pie has creamy undertones of coffee and a buttery frangipane layer.

FOR THE CHOCOLATE PASTRY

115 g/1 stick butter, chilled

240 g/1¾ cups plain/all-purpose flour, sifted, plus extra for dusting

40 g/generous ⅓ cup unsweetened cocoa powder, sifted

40 g/3 tablespoons caster/granulated sugar

2 egg yolks

FOR THE TOPPING

115 g/1 stick butter, softened

115 g/generous ½ cup caster/granulated sugar

2 eggs

115 g/½ cup ground almonds

30 g/3 tablespoons plain/all-purpose flour

1 teaspoon almond extract

50 g/⅓ cup plain/semisweet chocolate chips

4–5 tablespoons double/heavy cream

10 Marcona almonds, to decorate

50 g/2 oz. plain/semisweet chocolate, melted, to decorate

FOR THE CHOCOLATE FILLING

100 g/3½ oz. plain/semisweet chocolate

70 g/⅔ stick butter

2 eggs

80 g/6½ tablespoons caster/granulated sugar

125 ml/generous ½ cup double/heavy cream

1 shot espresso coffee

½ teaspoon salt

23-cm/9-in. loose-bottom, round, fluted tart pan, greased baking beans

Serves 10

For the pastry, rub the butter into the flour and cocoa with your fingertips. Add the sugar and egg yolks, and bring together into a soft dough, adding 1–2 tablespoons of cold water if needed. Wrap the pastry in clingfilm/plastic wrap and chill for 30 minutes in the refrigerator.

On a flour-dusted surface, roll the pastry out into a circle just larger than the size of your pan. Using the rolling pin to help lift it, carefully move the pastry into the pan and press it in. Trim the pastry so that there is just a little hanging over the sides of the pan. This will be trimmed neatly after cooking. Chill in the refrigerator for 30 minutes.

Preheat the oven to 200°C (400°F) Gas 6.

Line the pastry case with baking parchment and baking beans, and bake blind for 15–20 minutes, until the pastry is crisp. Remove from the oven and let cool. Reduce the oven temperature to 180°C (350°F) Gas 4. Once cool enough to handle, remove the baking beans and paper. Trim the edge of the pastry case with a sharp knife by running it along the top of the pan.

For the frangipane topping, whisk together the butter and sugar until light and creamy. Add the eggs, one at a time, whisking constantly. Fold in the ground almonds, flour, almond extract, chocolate chips and enough cream to make the mixture thick but easily spreadable. Set aside.

For the chocolate filling, melt the chocolate and butter in a heatproof bowl set over a saucepan of simmering water. Take care that the bottom of the bowl does not touch the water. Stir together to form a thick chocolate paste, then leave to cool slightly. In a separate bowl, whisk together the eggs and sugar until the mixture is thick and creamy, and has doubled in size. Carefully whisk in the chocolate mixture, cream, espresso and salt. Pour into the pie crust and bake for about 20 minutes, until the filling is just set but not cooked through.

Remove the chocolate tart from the oven and place spoonfuls of the frangipane mixture over the top of the pie. Using a knife, carefully spread the frangipane mixture over the top of the pie, then return to the oven and bake for a further 25–30 minutes, until golden brown on top. Remove from the oven and leave to cool completely.

To decorate the topping, dip the whole Marcona almonds partially in the melted chocolate and place in decorative patterns on top of the pie. This pie will keep for up to 3 days stored in an airtight container.

Salted caramel pie

If you love the classic combination of caramel and salt, then this is the pie for you. It has a thick layer of indulgent salted caramel sauce below a creamy custard layer, and is topped with caramel-flavoured chocolate.

FOR THE PIE CRUST

1 quantity shortcrust pastry (see page 9) or 500 g/18 oz. ready-made shortcrust pastry

plain/all-purpose flour, for dusting

FOR THE SALTED CARAMEL

100 g/7 tablespoons butter

100 g/½ cup caster/granulated sugar

1 teaspoon vanilla salt (or sea salt flakes)

400 g/14 oz. sweetened condensed milk

FOR THE CUSTARD

2 eggs

200 g/scant 1 cup cream cheese

200 ml/generous ¾ cup double/heavy cream

50 g/¼ cup caster/granulated sugar

TO DECORATE

50 g/2 oz. caramel-flavoured chocolate (such as Caramac)

23-cm/9-in. loose-bottom, round tart pan, greased

baking beans

Serves 10

On a flour-dusted surface, roll out the pastry thinly into a circle just larger than the size of your tart pan. Using the rolling pin to help lift it, carefully move the pastry into the pan and press it down so that it fits snugly. Trim away any excess pastry using a sharp knife, but leave some pastry hanging over the edge of the pan. This will be trimmed neatly after the tart is baked. Prick the base with a fork and chill in the refrigerator for 30 minutes.

Preheat the oven to 200°C (400°F) Gas 6.

Line the pastry with baking parchment, fill with baking beans and bake blind for about 15–20 minutes in the centre of the oven, until the pastry is golden brown. When cool enough to handle, remove the beans and baking parchment. Reduce the oven temperature to 180°C (350°F) Gas 4.

For the caramel layer, heat the butter and sugar in a saucepan with the salt, until the sugar has melted. Add the condensed milk and, stirring constantly, heat for about 5–10 minutes, until the sauce is thick and golden brown, taking care that the mixture does not burn. Spoon the mixture into the pie crust and leave to cool.

For the custard, whisk together the eggs, cream cheese, cream and sugar in a bowl until smooth. Gently pour over the caramel. Bake in the preheated oven for 40–50 minutes, until the top of the pie is lightly golden brown. Allow to cool, but not completely.

When the pie is almost cold, grate the caramel chocolate into curls with a vegetable peeler and sprinkle over the top of the pie. Leave the pie to cool completely. Trim the edge of the pastry case with a sharp knife by running it along the top of the pan. This pie will store for up to 3 days in the refrigerator.

Coffee cream pie

This pie contains a good dose of coffee! The bottom layer of the pie is a rich coffee ganache and this is then topped with creamy coffee mousse, whipped cream and the all-important chocolate coffee beans. Yum, yum!

FOR THE PIE CRUST

300 g/10½ oz. coffee-iced biscuits/cookies (such as Café Noir) or digestive biscuits/graham crackers

140 g/1¼ sticks butter, melted

FOR THE COFFEE GANACHE

1 egg

250 ml/generous 1 cup double/ heavy cream

1 small shot espresso coffee

150 g/5½ oz. dark/bittersweet chocolate (70% cocoa solids)

FOR THE COFFEE CREAM LAYER

2 sheets of platinum-grade leaf gelatine

100 ml/generous ⅓ cup double/heavy cream

5 tablespoons espresso coffee

250 g/generous 1 cup mascarpone cheese

50 g/¼ cup caster/superfine sugar

TO SERVE

200 ml/scant 1 cup double/heavy cream, whipped to stiff peaks

chocolate coffee beans

23-cm/9-in. loose-bottom, round tart pan, greased

piping/pastry bag fitted with star nozzle/tip

Serves 10

Blitz the cookies to fine crumbs in a food processor or place in a clean plastic bag and bash with a rolling pin. Stir in the melted butter so that all the crumbs are coated, then press into the base and sides of the pan firmly using the back of a spoon.

For the coffee ganache, whisk the egg, cream and coffee together. Break up chocolate into small pieces and place in a saucepan with the cream mixture. Heat over gentle heat, stirring constantly, for about 2–3 minutes, until the chocolate is melted and the ganache is thick and glossy. Pour into the pie crust and leave to chill in the refrigerator until set.

For the coffee cream layer, soak the gelatine in water until soft. Squeeze out the water and place in a heatproof bowl with the cream and coffee. Set the bowl over a saucepan of water and heat until the gelatine has melted. Whisk together the mascarpone and sugar and then pour over the warm cream, straining it through a sieve/strainer to remove any gelatine pieces. Whisk together until the cream is smooth. Carefully spoon the coffee cream over the chocolate ganache, then chill in the refrigerator for at least 3 hours or overnight, until the cream layer has set.

Spoon the whipped cream into a piping/pastry bag fitted with a star and then pipe stars of cream to decorate the pie. Decorate with the chocolate coffee beans to serve. This pie will keep for up to 3 days in the refrigerator.

Walnut custard tart

This is what I can only describe as a perfect family pie – filled with a creamy, nutty custard, it is simple and yet sophisticated enough to serve at any time of day, be it with coffee for elevenses or as a dinner-party dessert.

FOR THE PIE CRUST

1 quantity shortcrust pastry (see page 9) or 500 g/18 oz. ready-made shortcrust pastry

plain/all-purpose flour, for dusting

FOR THE FILLING

250 g/2 cups walnut pieces

1 tablespoon sunflower oil

2 tablespoons icing/confectioners' sugar

5 egg yolks

50 g/4 tablespoons caster/granulated sugar

50 g/4 tablespoons muscovado/molasses sugar

300 ml/1¼ cups double/heavy cream

1 teaspoon pure vanilla extract

23-cm/9-in. loose-bottom, round, fluted tart pan, greased

baking beans

Serves 8

On a flour-dusted surface, roll out the pastry thinly into a circle just larger than the size of your tart pan. Using the rolling pin to help lift it, carefully move the pastry into the pan and press it down so that it fits snugly. Trim away any excess pastry using a sharp knife, but leave some pastry hanging over the edge of the pan. This will be trimmed neatly after the tart is baked. Prick the base with a fork and chill in the refrigerator for 30 minutes.

Preheat the oven to 180°C (350°F) Gas 4.

Line the pastry with baking parchment, fill with baking beans and bake blind for about 15–20 minutes in the preheated oven, until the pastry is golden brown. When cool enough to handle, remove the parchment and beans. Trim the edge of the pastry to the level of the pan using a sharp knife.

Reduce the oven temperature to 150°C (300°F) Gas 2.

Chop one-fifth of the walnuts into small pieces and set aside. Blitz the remaining walnuts, oil and icing/confectioners' sugar together in a blender to a smooth paste. Whisk together the egg yolks, caster/granulated and muscovado/molasses sugars, until light and creamy. Slowly pour in the cream, vanilla and walnut paste and whisk well. Pour into the pie crust.

Sprinkle the chopped walnuts on top of the pie and bake for about 1 hour 30 minutes, until the top of the tart is golden brown and set with a slight wobble in the centre. Chill before serving. This tart will keep for up to 2 days in the refrigerator.

Prune and Armagnac tarts

Although prunes are not everyone's favourite fruit, when rehydrated with rich Armagnac they can't fail to delight. Baked in a light pastry crust, the creamy custard filling has the bitter sweetness of dark chocolate. This is a great tart to serve for dessert at dinner parties with a glass of Armagnac on the side.

FOR THE FILLING
250 g/9 oz. soft pitted prunes

100 ml/generous ⅓ cup Armagnac

150 g/1¼ sticks butter, softened

100 g/½ cup caster/ granulated sugar

100 g/½ cup soft dark brown sugar

200 g/2 cups ground almonds

150 g/generous 1 cup plain/ all-purpose flour, plus extra for dusting

3 eggs

100 g/3½ oz. plain/semisweet chocolate, chopped

FOR THE PASTRY
1 quantity shortcrust pastry (see page 9) or 500 g/18 oz. ready-made shortcrust pastry

TO DECORATE
icing/confectioners' sugar, for dusting

6 individual tartlet pans
baking beans

Serves 8

Reserve 18 prunes whole for the top of the tarts and chop the remainder into large pieces. Soak the prunes in the Armagnac for several hours until they are plump and juicy, pouring a little of the Armagnac onto the whole prunes and the remainder in a separate bowl onto the chopped prunes.

On a flour-dusted surface, roll out pastry thinly and line the pans with it. Press the pastry in firmly with your fingers and trim away any excess using a sharp knife, leaving some of the pastry hanging over the edge of the pans. You will trim the edge of the tarts after baking. Prick the base and chill in the refrigerator for 30 minutes.

Preheat the oven to 200°C (400°F) Gas 6.

Line the pastry cases with baking parchment, fill with baking beans and bake blind for about 10–15 minutes in the preheated oven, until the pastry is lightly golden brown. Reduce the oven temperature to 180°C (350°F) Gas 4. Once cool enough to handle, remove the parchment and baking beans. Trim the edge of the pastry to the level of the pans using a sharp knife.

For the frangipane, cream together the butter, caster/granulated sugar and soft dark brown sugar until very light and creamy. Add the eggs and whisk again until smooth. Add the ground almonds and flour and whisk in. Fold in the prune pieces, soaking Armagnac and chopped chocolate into the frangipane mixture, and spoon into the pie crusts, spreading out evenly. Decorate with the reserved prunes.

Bake for about 25–30 minutes, covering the frangipane with foil if it starts to brown too much towards the end of cooking. Serve with clotted or whipped cream and dust with a little icing/confectioners' sugar. These tarts will keep for up to 3 days stored in an airtight container.

Glazed cinnamon nut pie

This rich, buttery pie is packed with nuts and cinnamon, and is made with a sweet pastry. You can substitute any shelled, unsalted nuts of your choosing.

FOR THE PIE CRUST

115 g/1 stick butter, chilled

**280 g/generous 2 cups plain/
all-purpose flour, sifted,
plus extra for dusting**

**40 g/3¼ tablespoons caster/
granulated sugar**

2 egg yolks

1 teaspoon ground cinnamon

milk, for brushing

FOR THE FILLING

**150 g/generous 1 cup shelled
unsalted pistachios**

100 g/¾ cup blanched hazelnuts

150 g/1⅓ cups pecan halves

100 g/¾ cup blanched almonds

**200 g/1 cup caster/
granulated sugar**

**100 g/½ cup soft dark
brown sugar**

2 teaspoons ground cinnamon

1 teaspoon vanilla bean powder

**½ teaspoon vanilla salt
(or regular salt)**

100 g/7 tablespoons butter

**7 tablespoons golden/
light corn syrup**

3 eggs, beaten

FOR THE RUM CREAM

**300 ml/1¼ cups double/
heavy cream**

2 tablespoons dark rum

*23-cm/9-in. loose-bottom
pie dish, greased*

Serves 10

For the pastry, rub the butter into the flour with your fingertips. Add the sugar, egg yolks and cinnamon, and bring the mixture together into a soft dough, adding 1–2 tablespoons of cold water, if needed. Wrap the pastry in clingfilm/plastic wrap and chill in the refrigerator for 30 minutes.

On a flour-dusted surface, roll out the pastry thinly into a circle just larger than the size of your pie dish. Using the rolling pin to help lift it, carefully move the pastry into the dish and press it down so that it fits snugly. Trim away any excess pastry using a sharp knife, and use the trimmings to make leaf shapes to decorate the edge, if you like, brushing them with milk. Prick the base with a fork and chill in the refrigerator for 30 minutes.

Preheat the oven to 180°C (350°F) Gas 4.

For the filling, mix the nuts together and set aside enough whole nuts to cover the surface of your pie. These will be used to decorate the top of the pie. Blitz the remaining nuts to fine crumbs in the food processor, then pour into the chilled pie crust. Heat the caster/granulated sugar, soft dark brown sugar, cinnamon, vanilla powder, vanilla salt, butter and golden syrup in a saucepan over a gentle heat, until the sugar and butter have melted. Let cool.

Beat the eggs and whisk into the cooled syrup. Pass the syrup through a sieve/strainer and pour most of the syrup over the pecans, reserving a little for glazing. Arrange the whole nuts on top of the filling to decorate.

Bake in the preheated oven for 25 minutes, then turn the temperature down to 150°C (300°F) Gas 2 and bake for a further 10–15 minutes, until the pie is set with a slight wobble. Remove from the oven and brush over the remaining syrup to glaze. Leave to cool before serving.

For the rum cream, place the cream and rum in a mixing bowl and whip to soft peaks. Serve with the pie. The pie will store for up to 3 days in an airtight container.

Chocolate pistachio pie

My friend Gavin Gant loves this pie and is always asking me to make it. The pistachio custard is made with homemade pistachio paste and is baked in a rich chocolate-cookie crust. It has a beautiful pale-green colour and is decorated with vibrant green pistachios.

FOR THE PIE CRUST

250 g/9 oz. chocolate sandwich cookies, such as Oreos

115 g/1 stick butter, melted

2 tablespoons caster/granulated sugar

½ teaspoon vanilla salt (or regular salt)

FOR THE PISTACHIO PASTE

200 g/1½ cups shelled, unsalted pistachios

2 tablespoons flavourless oil, such as vegetable or sunflower

1 heaped tablespoon icing/confectioners' sugar

FOR THE FILLING

200 g/scant 1 cup cream cheese

140 g/scant ¾ cup caster/granulated sugar

3 eggs

250 ml/generous 1 cup double/ heavy cream

TO DECORATE

50 g/2 oz. plain/semisweet chocolate, melted

finely chopped shelled, unsalted pistachios

23-cm/9-in. loose-bottom, round fluted tart pan, greased

Serves 10

Blitz the cookies to fine crumbs in a food processor or blender, or place in a clean plastic bag and bash with a rolling pin. Stir in the melted butter then press into the base and sides of the pan firmly, so that the sides have a thick layer of crumbs on and the base is completely covered, with no gaps. Chill in the refrigerator for 30 minutes.

To make the pistachio paste, place the pistachios, oil and icing/confectioners' sugar in a food processor or blender and blitz to a smooth paste. Let cool, as the mixture will become warm during blending.

Preheat the oven to 180°C (350°F) Gas 4.

For the filling, whisk together the cooled pistachio paste, cream cheese, sugar and eggs. Pour in the cream and whisk until smooth.

Wrap the base and sides of the chilled tart pan in foil to catch any butter that may be released during baking, and place it on a baking sheet. Pour the filling into the pie crust and carefully transfer to the preheated oven. Bake for 40–50 minutes, until the custard is just set.

Let the pie cool. The filling will have risen during baking and will sink back within the case as the pie cools.

Using a fork, drizzle melted chocolate around the edge of the pie and sprinkle with finely chopped pistachios. Chill until serving. This pie will store for up to 3 days in a refrigerator.

Malted mascarpone pie

I love the flavour of malt. It is one of the most comforting tastes and this is the pie I make when I need a little pick-me-up. Topped with whipped cream and Maltesers/Whoppers, this is a great party pie and is always popular. If you can't find malted milks, replace with digestive biscuits or graham crackers.

FOR THE PIE CRUST

250 g/9 oz. malted milk biscuits/ cookies or digestive biscuits/ graham crackers

100 g/7 tablespoons butter, melted

a pinch of salt

2 tablespoons caster/ granulated sugar

FOR THE FILLING

250 g/generous 1 cup mascarpone cheese

300 ml/1¼ cups double/ heavy cream

3 eggs, beaten

100 g/½ cup caster/ granulated sugar

80 g/2¾ oz. malt drink powder, such as Horlicks/Ovaltine

FOR THE TOPPING

250 ml/generous 1 cup double/ heavy cream

chocolate-coated malt balls, such as Maltesers/Whoppers

unsweetened cocoa powder, for dusting

23-cm/9-in. loose-bottom, round, fluted tart pan, greased

Serves 10

Blitz the cookies to fine crumbs in a food processor or place in a clean plastic bag and bash with a rolling pin. Stir in the melted butter, salt and sugar, then press into the base and sides of the pan firmly, so that the sides have a thick layer of crumbs on and the base is completely covered with no gaps. Chill in the refrigerator for 30 minutes.

Preheat the oven to 180°C (350°F) Gas 4.

For the filling, whisk together the mascarpone cheese, cream, eggs, sugar and malt powder until smooth and creamy. Wrap the base and sides of the pan in foil and place on a baking sheet to catch any butter that is released during cooking. Pour the filling into the pie crust and carefully transfer to the preheated oven. Bake for 40–50 minutes, until the custard is just set with a slight wobble in the centre.

Remove from the oven and let cool. The custard will sink back down into the pie crust as it cools.

Whip the cream to soft peaks and spoon on top of the pie in gentle peaks. Cut the chocolate-coated malt balls into pieces using a sharp knife and sprinkle over the top of the pie. Dust with cocoa powder and serve immediately or store in the refrigerator until serving.

This pie is best eaten on the day it is made. However, it can be stored for up to 2 days in the refrigerator, as long as you add the topping just before serving it.

Raspberry and rose tartlets

These dainty pies are perfect to serve for afternoon tea or as an elegant dessert. The tart cases are lined with a thin layer of dark/bittersweet chocolate, which offers the perfect foil to the sharpness of the fruit.

FOR THE PASTRY

60 g/4 tablespoons butter, chilled

140 g/1 cup plain/all-purpose flour, sifted

a pinch of salt

FOR THE CRÈME PATISSIÈRE

1 tablespoon cornflour/cornstarch

1 tablespoon rosewater

60 g/⅓ cup caster/granulated sugar

1 egg and 1 egg yolk

100 ml/1⅓ cups full-fat/whole milk

150 ml/⅔ cup double/heavy cream

TO ASSEMBLE

50 g/⅓ cup dark/bittersweet chocolate, melted

250 g/2 cups raspberries

chopped pistachios

FOR THE GLAZE

3 tablespoons apricot glaze

12-hole fluted muffin pan, greased
9-cm/3½-in. round cookie cutter
piping/pastry bag fitted with large star nozzle/tip

Makes 12

For the pastry, rub the butter into the flour and salt using your fingertips. Add 1 tablespoon of cold water and mix in with a round-bladed knife, adding a little more water if the mixture is too dry. Wrap the pastry in clingfilm/plastic wrap and chill in the refrigerator for 1 hour.

On a flour-dusted surface, roll out the pastry dough thinly and cut out 12 circles using the cutter. Press one circle into each of the holes of the muffin pan. Prick the base of each pie and chill in the refrigerator for a further 30 minutes.

Preheat the oven to 200°C (400°F) Gas 6.

Line the pastry cases with baking parchment, fill with baking beans and bake blind for about 10–15 minutes in the centre of the oven, until the pastry is golden brown. Let cool and remove the baking beans and parchment, then brush the insides of the pastry cases with a thin layer of melted chocolate. Let set.

To prepare the crème patissière, whisk together the cornflour/cornstarch, rosewater, sugar, egg and egg yolk until creamy. Put the milk and cream in a saucepan and bring to the boil. Pour over the egg mixture immediately, whisking all the time. Return to the pan and cook for a few minutes, until thick. Pass through a sieve/strainer to remove any lumps and let cool.

To assemble, spoon the rose crème patissière into a piping/pastry bag fitted with a large round nozzle/tip and pipe into the cases. Top with the raspberries and chopped pistachios.

To glaze, heat the apricot glaze in a saucepan until just melted, cool slightly and then brush over the raspberries using a pastry brush.

Hazelnut croquant pie

This rich and indulgent pie is made with layers of chocolate hazelnut mousse and hazelnut meringues, and topped with cream and hazelnut praline.

FOR THE MERINGUE LAYERS
2 egg whites
115 g/generous ½ cup caster/superfine sugar
100 g/scant 1 cup chopped roasted hazelnuts

FOR THE PIE CRUST
300 g/10½ oz. digestive biscuits/graham crackers
50 g/scant ½ cup chopped roasted hazelnuts
125 g/9 tablespoons butter, melted

FOR THE MOUSSE
200 g/7 oz. dark/bittersweet chocolate (85% cocoa solids), melted and cooled
150 ml/⅔ cup double/heavy cream
1 heaped tablespoon chocolate hazelnut spread, such as Nutella
2 egg whites
1 tablespoon caster/superfine sugar

TO DECORATE
80 g/scant ½ cup caster/superfine sugar
50 g/⅓ cup roasted hazelnuts
250 ml/generous 1 cup double/heavy cream

3 large baking sheets lined with silicone mats or baking parchment
25-cm/10-in. round springform cake pan, greased and lined

Serves 12

Preheat the oven to 140°C (275°F) Gas 1.

For the meringue layers, whisk the egg whites to stiff peaks, then add the sugar a spoonful at a time, whisking constantly, until the meringue is smooth, thick and glossy. Gently fold in the hazelnuts using a spatula. Spread the meringue out on 2 of the prepared baking sheets in 2 circles, approximately 22 cm/8½ in. in diameter. Bake for 1–1¼ hours, until the meringues are crisp. Let cool.

Blitz the biscuits/crackers to fine crumbs in a food processor or blender, or place in a clean plastic bag and bash with a rolling pin. Stir in the hazelnuts and melted butter until everything is well mixed and all the crumbs are coated in butter. Press into the base and sides of the pan firmly, so that the sides have a thick layer of crumbs on and the base is completely covered, with no gaps. Chill in the refrigerator for 30 minutes.

For the mousse, fold the cooled melted chocolate into the cream and whisk together with the chocolate hazelnut spread until the cream thickens. Whisk the egg whites to stiff peaks, then add the sugar while still whisking. Fold the chocolate mixture into the egg whites gently with a spatula.

Spoon one-third of the mousse into the pie crust and spread out evenly. Place one of the meringues on top and then cover with a further third of the mousse. Place the second meringue on top and cover with the remaining mousse. Chill in the refrigerator for at least 3 hours.

For the hazelnut praline, heat the sugar in a saucepan until it melts, swirling the pan to prevent the sugar from burning. Do not stir with a spoon. You need to watch very carefully as the sugar melts, as it can burn very easily. Spread the hazelnuts out on the third silicone mat or baking sheet and then pour over the melted sugar. Let cool, then break it up into chunks. Keep half of the praline in chunks and blitz the rest to small pieces in a food processor or blender.

Whip the cream to stiff peaks and spoon in peaks over the top of the pie. Sprinkle with the small and large pieces of hazelnut praline and serve immediately. This pie will store for up to 2 days in the refrigerator, but the praline is best added just before serving.

Family treats

Mississippi mud pie

Cookie dough pie

Treacle tart

Honeycomb pie

Chocolate caramel crunch tart

Chocolate brownie pie

Peanut pie

Banoffee pie

Ice cream pie

Baked Alaska pies

Mississippi mud pie

I remember learning how to spell Mississippi at school with the "Mrs M, Mrs I, Mrs SSI" chant, but at the time I had no idea that one of my future favourite desserts would originate from the same place. It is meant to resemble the muddy swamp base, but fear not — there is no mud — just delicious chocolate!

FOR THE SHORTBREAD

200 g/1½ cups plain/
all-purpose flour

40 g/generous ⅓ cup
unsweetened cocoa powder

a pinch of salt

60 g/5 tablespoons caster/
granulated sugar

160 g/1½ sticks butter

1–2 tablespoons milk (optional)

FOR THE FILLING

150 g/5½ oz. plain/semisweet
chocolate

100 g/7 tablespoons butter

3 eggs

60 g/5 tablespoons muscovado/
molasses sugar

60 g/5 tablespoons caster/
granulated sugar

175 ml/¾ cup double/
heavy cream

TO DECORATE

250 ml/generous 1 cup double/
heavy cream

chocolate popping candy
or chocolate sprinkles

*23-cm/9-in. loose-bottom, round,
fluted tart pan, greased
baking beans*

Serves 8–10

For the shortbread base, sift together the flour and cocoa powder, and stir in the salt and sugar. Cut the butter into cubes and rub into the flour mixture until the mixture resembles fine breadcrumbs. Bring the dough together into a ball. If the mixture is too crumbly, add a little milk.

Press the dough into the base and sides of your pan evenly using your fingertips. Chill in the freezer for 30 minutes.

Preheat the oven to 200°C (400°F) Gas 6.

Line the shortbread with baking parchment and fill with baking beans. Bake for 15–20 minutes, until cooked through, then remove the baking beans and parchment, and let cool.

Reduce the oven temperature to 180°C (350°F) Gas 4.

For the chocolate filling, melt the chocolate and butter in a heatproof bowl set over a saucepan of simmering water. Take care that the bottom of the bowl does not touch the water. Stir together to form a thick chocolate ganache, then leave to cool slightly.

In a separate bowl, whisk together the eggs, muscovado/molasses and caster/granulated sugars until thick and creamy and the mixture has doubled in size. Carefully whisk in the chocolate mixture and the cream. Pour into the prepared shortbread pie crust and bake in the preheated oven for 30–40 minutes, until the filling is just set but still has a slight wobble in the centre. Let cool.

To decorate, whip the cream to soft peaks and spread over the top of the pie. Decorate with chocolate popping candy or chocolate sprinkles. Store in the refrigerator for up to 2 days if you are not eating it immediately.

Cookie dough pie

For someone who loves ice-cold milk and cookies, this is one of my favourite pies. The crust is a giant cookie and the filling a baked custard sweetened with chocolate chips and condensed milk containing soft cookie-dough balls. Serve this pie chilled with glasses of milk as a perfect midnight-feast treat.

FOR THE COOKIE CRUST

60 g/5 tablespoons caster/granulated sugar

115 g/1 stick butter, softened

170 g/1¼ cups plain/all-purpose flour, sifted

1 teaspoon pure vanilla extract

100 g/⅔ cup chocolate chips (a mix of white, milk and plain/semisweet of your choosing)

FOR THE FILLING

200 g/scant 1 cup cream cheese

200 g/7 oz. sweetened condensed milk

3 eggs

200 ml/generous ¾ cup double/heavy cream

1 teaspoon pure vanilla extract

150 g/1 cup chocolate chips (a mix of white, milk and plain/semisweet of your choosing)

23-cm/9-in. loose-bottom, round, fluted tart pan, greased

baking beans

Serves 10

For the cookie crust, whisk together the sugar and butter until creamy. Add the flour and vanilla extract, and whisk again. The mixture should form large clumps of dough. Add the chocolate chips and bring the dough together into a ball with your hands, adding a little water if the mixture is too crumbly.

Set aside about one-quarter of the dough to make the cookie-dough balls, then press the rest of the dough into the pan with your fingertips, so that it forms a thin layer around the sides and over the base of the pan. Chill in the refrigerator for 1 hour.

Roll the reserved cookie dough into about 15 small balls and place in the freezer until you are ready to cook the pie filling.

Preheat the oven to 180°C (350°F) Gas 4. Line the cookie crust with baking parchment and fill with baking beans. Bake for 15–20 minutes, until the cookie is just cooked (it will cook further while the filling is cooking). Let cool, then remove the parchment and baking beans.

For the filling, whisk together the cream cheese, condensed milk and eggs. Pour in the cream, and whisk until the mixture is smooth. Fold in the vanilla extract and chocolate chips, and pour the filling into the case, until it is just below the rim of the cookie crust. Remove the cookie-dough balls from the freezer and distribute evenly in the pie filling.

Bake for 40–50 minutes in the preheated oven, until the custard is just set but still has a slight wobble in the centre. Let cool. The filling will have risen during baking and will sink back within the case as the pie cools. This pie will keep for up to 3 days in the refrigerator.

Treacle tart

This naughty dessert reminds me of school dinners – treacle tart day was one we really looked forward to. There are so many different ways to make treacle tart, but I like mine to have plenty of lemon, as I find this cuts through the sweetness of the syrup. However, you can use less lemon juice, if you prefer.

FOR THE PIE CRUST

1 quantity shortcrust pastry
(see page 9) or 500 g/18 oz.
ready-made shortcrust pastry

plain/all-purpose flour,
for dusting

FOR THE FILLING

2 lemons

200 g/7 oz. sliced white
bread (about 6–8 slices)

400 g/1¼ cups golden/
light corn syrup

80 g/¾ stick butter

1 egg, beaten

caster/granulated sugar,
for sprinkling

23-cm/9-in. loose-bottom, round,
fluted tart pan, greased

baking beans

small heart cutter

Serves 8

On a flour-dusted surface, roll out the pastry thinly into a circle just larger than the size of your tart pan. Using the rolling pin to help lift it, carefully move the pastry into the pan and press it down so that it fits snugly. Trim away any excess pastry using a sharp knife, but leave some pastry hanging over the edge of the pan. This will be trimmed neatly after the tart is baked. Prick the base with a fork and chill in the refrigerator for 30 minutes.

Roll out the pastry trimmings and cut out about 15–20 heart shapes. Reserve these for decoration.

Preheat the oven to 200°C (400°F) Gas 6.

Line the pastry case with baking parchment and fill with baking beans. Bake the pastry for 10–15 minutes in the preheated oven, until lightly golden brown, then remove from the oven and let cool. Remove the beans and parchment. Trim the edge of the pastry to the height of the pan using a sharp knife. Reduce the oven temperature to 190°C (375°C) Gas 5.

Zest one of the lemons and add the zest to a food processor along with the bread, and blitz to fine crumbs.

In a saucepan, heat the syrup, butter and juice of both of the lemons, until the butter has melted. Let cool slightly.

Place the breadcrumbs into the pastry case and pour over the cooled syrup. Stir the mixture carefully with a fork to ensure that all the crumbs are coated in syrup.

Place the pastry hearts on top of the filling in a decorative pattern around the edge, and brush with a little beaten egg. Sprinkle the hearts with sugar.

Bake the tart for 15 minutes in the preheated oven, then reduce the temperature to 180°C (350°F) Gas 4 and bake for 10–15 minutes more, until the pastry is golden brown and the filling has risen and is set with a slight wobble.

Serve warm or cold with custard or cream. This tart will keep well for 3 days stored in an airtight container.

Honeycomb pie

This pie contains the popular confection chocolate-covered honeycomb/sponge candy. It has a layer of chocolate ganache, is topped with a rich vanilla custard and finished with pieces of the golden, crunchy candy.

FOR THE PIE CRUST

1 quantity shortcrust pastry (see page 9) or 500 g/18 oz. ready-made shortcrust pastry

plain/all-purpose flour, for dusting

FOR THE GANACHE

200 g/7 oz. dark/bittersweet chocolate, 85% cocoa solids

120 ml/½ cup double/ heavy cream

50 g/3½ tablespoons butter

FOR THE CUSTARD TOPPING

5 egg yolks

75 g/6 tablespoons caster/ granulated sugar

375 ml/generous 1½ cups double/heavy cream

½ teaspoon vanilla bean powder or 1 teaspoon pure vanilla extract

90 g/3 oz. chocolate-covered honeycomb, crushed, such as Cadbury's Crunchie/Watson's Sponge Candy

20 x 30-cm/8 x 12-in. loose-bottom, rectangular, fluted, tart pan

baking beans

Serves 12

On a flour-dusted surface, roll out the pastry thinly into a rectangle just larger than the size of your tart pan. Using the rolling pin to help lift it, carefully move the pastry into the pan and press it down so that it fits snugly. Trim away any excess pastry using a sharp knife, but leave some pastry hanging over the edge of the pan. This will be trimmed neatly after the tart is baked. Prick the base with a fork and chill in the refrigerator for 30 minutes.

Preheat the oven to 200°C (400°F) Gas 6. Line the pie crust with baking parchment, fill with baking beans and bake blind for about 20–25 minutes in the centre of the preheated oven, until the pastry is lightly golden brown. Remove from the oven and, once cool enough to handle, remove the baking beans and parchment. The pastry will cook further whilst the filling is cooking. Carefully trim the pastry using a sharp knife, so that it is level with the top of the pan.

Reduce the oven temperature to 150°C (300°F) Gas 2.

For the ganache, place the chocolate, cream and butter in a heatproof bowl set over a pan of simmering water and heat until the chocolate and butter have melted. Stir well, so that the cream, chocolate and butter blend together and you have a thick, glossy sauce. Spread over the base of the pie crust.

For the custard, whisk together the egg yolks and sugar until thick and creamy. Slowly pour in the cream, whisking all the time. Whisk in the vanilla powder or vanilla extract. Carefully pour the custard over the chocolate layer. Sprinkle the top of the custard with the crushed chocolate-covered honeycomb.

Bake in the oven for 1–1¼ hours, until the custard layer has set but still has a slight wobble in the centre. Chill before serving. This pie will keep for up to 3 days in the refrigerator.

Chocolate caramel crunch tart

If you like toffee and caramel, then this is the pie for you. It has a caramel-flavoured cookie crust, caramel custard and is topped with crunchy pieces of Daim bar, which is similar to a US Heath bar. This pie is wicked!

FOR THE PIE CRUST

250 g/9 oz. caramel biscuits/cookies, such as Lotus

115 g/1 stick butter, melted

FOR THE FILLING

250 g/generous 1 cup mascarpone cheese

300 ml/1¼ cup sour cream

3 eggs

400 g/14 oz. caramel or dulce de leche sauce

FOR THE TOPPING

4 Daim/Heath bars

23-cm/9-in. loose-bottom, round, fluted tart pan, greased

Serves 10

Preheat the oven to 170°C (325°F) Gas 3.

Blitz the cookies to fine crumbs in a food processor or blender, or place in a clean plastic bag and bash with a rolling pin. Add the melted butter and mix well so that all the crumbs are coated in butter. Using the back of a spoon, press the cookie crumb mixture into the prepared pan so that the sides have a thick layer of crumbs on and the base is completely covered, with no gaps.

For the filling, whisk together the mascarpone cheese, sour cream, eggs and caramel until smooth and creamy. Wrap the base and sides of the pan in foil and place on a baking sheet to catch any butter that might be released during baking. Pour the filling into the pie crust and carefully transfer to the oven.

Bake for 40–45 minutes in the preheated oven, until the custard is just set with a slight wobble in the centre. Remove from the oven and let cool. The custard will sink back down into the pie crust as it cools.

As soon as the pie is taken out of the oven, chop the Daim/Heath bars into small pieces and sprinkle over the top of the pie. The chocolate on the Daim/Heath bar pieces will melt onto the pie. Chill before serving. This pie will keep for up to 3 days stored in the refrigerator.

Chocolate brownie pie

This recipe combines two of my favourite things – Oreo cookies and chocolate brownies – in one very indulgent pie. It is important not to over-cook the pie, so that the brownie filling is still deliciously gooey when cooled. The shot of espresso really makes the chocolate flavours sing.

FOR THE PIE CRUST

250 g/9 oz. chocolate sandwich cookies, such as Oreos

100 g/7 tablespoons butter, melted

FOR THE BROWNIE FILLING

200 g/7 oz. dark/bittersweet chocolate

125 g/9 tablespoons butter

2 UK large/US extra-large eggs

100 g/½ cup caster/ granulated sugar

100 g/½ cup muscovado/ molasses sugar

1 small shot of espresso coffee

100 g/¾ cup plain/ all-purpose flour

1 teaspoon vanilla bean powder or pure vanilla extract

100 g/3½ oz. white chocolate, chopped

unsweetened cocoa powder, for dusting

23-cm/9-in. loose-bottom, round, fluted tart pan, greased

Serves 8–10

For the pie crust, blitz the cookies to fine crumbs in a food processor or blender, or place in a clean plastic bag and bash with a rolling pin. Add the melted butter and mix well so that all the crumbs are coated in butter. Using the back of a spoon, press the cookie crumb mixture into the prepared pan so that the sides have a thick layer of crumbs to hold the filling and the base is completely covered, with no gaps. Wrap the base and sides of the pan in foil to catch any butter that may be released during baking.

Preheat the oven to 180°C (350°F) Gas 4.

For the brownie filling, place the chocolate and butter in a heatproof bowl set over a pan of simmering water until both have melted, stirring occasionally. If it is more convenient, you can do this in a microwave instead: heat on full power for 1 minute, stir and then heat for a further 20 seconds or until both the butter and chocolate have melted. Let cool.

In a clean bowl whisk together the eggs, caster/granulated and muscovado/molasses sugars until the mixture is thick and creamy and a pale yellow colour. Pour in the chocolate mixture and espresso, and whisk in. Add the flour and vanilla powder, and fold in gently using a spatula. Pour the mixture into the prepared pie crust.

Bake in the preheated oven for 25–30 minutes, until a crust has formed on top of the brownie but the brownie still feels soft underneath. About 10 minutes before the end of cooking time, sprinkle the chopped white chocolate pieces over the top of the pie, as they will melt during the final cooking. Allow to cool and set before serving dusted with cocoa powder. This pie will keep well for up to 3 days stored in an airtight container.

Peanut pie

This is a rich and indulgent pie bursting with peanuts. The crust is made from peanut cookies, but if you do not have them you can use regular digestives/graham crackers and add a handful of sweet honey-roasted peanuts to the blender when blitzing the cookies for equally delicious results.

FOR THE PIE CRUST

400 g/14 oz. peanut cookies

150 g/1¼ sticks butter

FOR THE FILLING

200 g/scant 1 cup full-fat cream cheese

150 g/¾ cup caster/granulated sugar

3 eggs

120 g/generous ½ cup crunchy peanut butter

250 ml/generous 1 cup double/heavy cream

4 nutty caramel nougat bars, such as Snickers bars

23-cm/9-in. loose-bottom fluted tart pan, greased

Serves 10

For the pie crust, blitz the cookies to fine crumbs in a food processor or blender, or place in a clean plastic bag and bash with a rolling pin. Add the melted butter and mix well so that all the crumbs are coated in butter. Using the back of a spoon, press the cookie crumb mixture into the prepared pan so that the sides have a thick layer of crumbs on and the base is completely covered, with no gaps. Chill the pie crust in the refrigerator for 30 minutes.

Preheat the oven to 180°C (350°F) Gas 4.

For the filling, whisk together the cream cheese, sugar, eggs and peanut butter. Pour in the cream and whisk until smooth. Wrap the base and sides of the pan in foil to catch any butter that may be released during baking, and place on a baking sheet. Pour the filling into the pie crust. Cut the nutty caramel nougat bars into pieces and place at intervals into the filling. Carefully transfer to the preheated oven.

Bake for 40–50 minutes, until the filling is just set. Let cool. The filling will have risen during baking and will sink back into the case as the pie cools. Chill in the refrigerator, then serve cold. The pie will keep for up to 3 days stored in the refrigerator.

Banoffee pie

Everyone loves banoffee pie — it is a quick and easy dessert to prepare and is always popular. Filled with buttery caramel and lemon-soaked bananas, and topped with chocolate curls and cream, this is delicious pie for banana lovers.

FOR THE PIE CRUST

300 g/10½ oz. digestive biscuits/ graham crackers

150 g/1¼ sticks butter, melted

FOR THE CARAMEL LAYER

90 g/scant ½ cup muscovado/ molasses sugar

30 g/2½ tablespoons caster/ granulated sugar

100 g/1 stick minus 1 tablespoon butter

400 g/14 oz. can of sweetened condensed milk

a pinch of salt

TO ASSEMBLE

3 bananas

freshly squeezed juice of 1 lemon

400 ml/scant 1¾ cups double/heavy cream

50 g/2 oz. plain/semisweet chocolate

25-cm/10-in. springform cake pan, greased and lined

Serves 8–10

Blitz the digestive biscuits/graham crackers to fine crumbs in a food processor or blender, or place in a clean plastic bag and bash with a rolling pin. Add the melted butter and stir well until all the crumbs are coated. Press the crumbs into the sides and base of pan, so that the crumbs come about 4 cm/1½ in. up the sides and will hold the filling. Press a pattern of indents into the edge using your thumb, if you like.

Heat the muscovado/molasses and caster/granulated sugars in a saucepan with the butter, until the sugars and butter have melted. Add the condensed milk and salt, and stir over a gentle heat for about 10 minutes until you have a thick caramel, stirring all the time to ensure the caramel does not burn. Pour into the pie crust and let cool.

When you are ready to serve, peel the bananas and cut into slices, and coat with the lemon juice to prevent them from browning. Place the bananas on top of the caramel. Whip the cream to soft peaks. Spoon the cream over the bananas and caramel, making sure that all the bananas are covered. Using a swivel peeler, make chocolate curls and sprinkle over the top of the pie. This pie will keep for up to 2 days if stored in the refrigerator.

Ice cream pie

This pie is completely kitsch and quirky. You can make it with any flavour of ice cream – or why not try mixing different flavours for a two-tone pie. As the pie contains ice cream it is important to work quickly and place it in the freezer as soon as possible for best results.

FOR THE PIE CRUST

250 g/9 oz. digestive biscuits/ graham crackers

100 g/7 tablespoons butter, melted

FOR THE FILLING

500 ml/16 fl oz. ice cream (flavour of your choosing)

300 ml/1¼ cups double/ heavy cream

TO DECORATE

50 g/2 oz. plain/semisweet chocolate, melted and cooled

chocolate confections

23-cm/9-in. deep pie dish, greased

Serves 6

Blitz the digestive biscuits/graham crackers to fine crumbs in a food processor or blender, or place in a clean plastic bag and bash with a rolling pin. Stir in the melted butter, ensuring that all the crumbs are well coated. Press the crumbs into the base and sides of the pie dish using the back of a spoon. Place the pie crust in the freezer and chill for 30 minutes. It is important to do this so that the case is cold, which will help prevent the ice-cream mixture from melting.

For the filling, bring the ice cream just to room temperature, until it is soft enough to spoon out. Gently whip the double/heavy cream to soft peaks, then beat in the ice cream quickly. Working very fast, spoon the ice-cream mixture into the frozen pie crust and transfer immediately to the freezer. Leave until the filling is frozen completely.

To decorate, drizzle the frozen pie with the cooled melted chocolate and fix chocolate confections on top with a little chocolate. You need to work quickly, as the chocolate will set very quickly on the frozen ice cream. It is also important that the melted chocolate is cooled; if it is drizzled while hot, it will melt the ice cream. Return the pie to the freezer immediately and freeze until you are ready to serve.

When you want to eat the pie, bring it to room temperature and then serve in large slices to your guests. This pie will keep for up to a month, wrapped in clingfilm/plastic wrap, in the freezer.

Baked Alaska pies

Caramel Alaskas are perfect party pies — with a caramel pastry case, caramel ice cream and toffee sauce. These hot and cold desserts needs only one thing — giant forks or spoons to dig in with.

FOR THE SHORTBREAD

220 g/1²⁄₃ cups plain/all-purpose flour, sifted

a pinch of salt

60 g/5 tablespoons soft dark brown sugar

½ teaspoon vanilla bean powder or 1 teaspoon vanilla extract

150 g/1¼ sticks butter, softened

FOR THE CARAMEL SAUCE

50 g/¼ cup soft dark brown sugar

50 g/¼ cup caster/ granulated sugar

100 g/7 tablespoons butter

250 ml/generous 1 cup double/ heavy cream

FOR THE ALASKA TOPPING

200 g/1 cup caster/ superfine sugar

3 egg whites

TO ASSEMBLE

about 450 ml/15 fl oz. caramel or toffee ice cream

six 10-cm/4-in. loose-bottom, round, fluted tartlet pans, greased

baking beans

piping/pastry bag fitted with a large star nozzle/tip (optional)

chef's blow torch

Serves 6

For the shortbread, place the flour, salt, sugar and vanilla in a bowl. Mix the butter into the flour mixture to form a soft dough. Press the dough out into the pans so that it goes up the sides and base of each pan. Press out thinly with your fingertips. Chill in the refrigerator for 1 hour.

Preheat the oven to 180°C (350°F) Gas 4.

Line the shortbread with baking parchment and fill with baking beans. Bake the shortbread base for 20–25 minutes, until golden brown. Leave in the pan to cool, then remove the parchment and beans.

Next prepare the caramel sauce. Heat the brown and white sugars in a saucepan with the butter until the sugar has melted. Remove the pan from the heat and cool for a few minutes, then whisk in the cream. Return the pan to the heat and boil gently for a few minutes until the sauce thickens. Leave to cool completely.

When you are ready to serve, prepare the Alaska topping. Heat the sugar with 60 ml/4 tablespoons of water in a saucepan and bring to the boil. Whisk the egg whites to stiff peaks and then add the hot sugar syrup in a steady stream, slowly whisking all the time. The hot sugar syrup will cook the eggs. Whisk for about 3–5 minutes, until the meringue is stiff.

Now you need to work quickly to prevent the ice cream from melting. Place each pie crust on a serving plate and fill with scoops of the ice cream. Drizzle with a little of the cooled caramel sauce, then spoon or pipe the meringue over the top in swirled peaks. Toast the outside of the meringue with the blow torch until golden brown and caramelized, then serve immediately so that your guests can enjoy the hot/cold effect of the Alaska. Serve with the remaining caramel sauce to pour over – either hot or cold. This pie needs to be eaten straight away and will not keep.

Global

Black Forest tart

Tarte au citron

Boston cream pie

Crème brûlée tarts

Scandinavian cardamom cream pie

Tiramisù pie

Portuguese custard tarts

Kentish pudding pie

Piña colada pie

Black Forest tart

This rich indulgent tart is inspired by the classic German cake Black Forest Gâteau, with kirsch-soaked cherries, a delicious chocolate shortbread and a chocolate ganache. This is a special tart that is perfect for afternoon tea.

FOR THE SHORTBREAD BASE

190 g/scant 1½ cups plain/all-purpose flour

40 g/generous ⅓ cup unsweetened cocoa powder

a pinch of salt

60 g/5 tablespoons caster/granulated sugar

150 g/1¼ sticks butter, softened

FOR THE FILLING

390 g/14 oz. cherries in kirsch, drained (approx 250 g/9 oz. drained weight)

2 eggs

375 ml/generous 1½ cups double/heavy cream

125 ml/scant ½ cup milk

300 g/10½ oz. dark/bittersweet chocolate (70% cocoa solids)

a pinch of vanilla salt (or regular salt)

TO SERVE

250 ml/generous 1 cup double/heavy cream

200 g/1⅓ cups fresh cherries

50 g/2 oz. dark/bittersweet chocolate, grated into curls with a peeler

23-cm/9-in. loose-bottom, round, fluted tart pan, greased

baking beans

Serves 14

For the shortbread base, sift the flour and cocoa powder together. Add the salt and sugar, and stir together. Mix the butter into the flour mixture to form a soft dough. Press out the dough with your fingertips into the pan so that it goes up the sides and base of the pan. Chill in the refrigerator for 1 hour.

Preheat the oven to 180°C (350°F) Gas 4.

Line the shortbread with baking parchment and fill with baking beans. Bake for 20–25 minutes, until the shortbread is cooked. Remove the baking beans and parchment, and let cool.

Spread the drained cherries over the base of the pie.

Whisk together the eggs, cream and milk. Break the chocolate up into small pieces and place in a saucepan with the egg mixture and salt. Cook over a gentle heat, stirring constantly, for about 4–5 minutes, until chocolate has melted and the ganache is thick and glossy. Pour into the pie crust, over the cherries, and leave to chill in the refrigerator for several hours or, ideally, overnight.

When you are ready to serve, whip the cream to soft peaks and spoon over the top of the pie. Top with the fresh cherries and sprinkle with the chocolate curls. Serve immediately or store in the refrigerator until you are ready to eat. This pie will keep for up to 2 days in the refrigerator, although should ideally only be topped with the cream just before serving for best results.

Tarte au citron

Lemon tart is a classic French pâtisserie delight. It has a sharp citrus flavour and makes a delicious treat served with fresh blueberries and a little cream.

FOR THE PIE CRUST

1 quantity shortcrust pastry (see page 9) or 500 g/18 oz. ready-made shortcrust pastry

plain/all-purpose flour, for dusting

FOR THE CUSTARD

8 eggs

300 g/1½ cups caster/granulated sugar

grated zest and freshly squeezed juice of 4 lemons

freshly squeezed juice of 2 limes

300 ml/1¼ cups double/heavy cream

FOR DECORATION

icing/confectioners' sugar, for dusting

23-cm/9-in. loose-bottom, round, fluted tart pan, greased

baking beans

chef's blow torch

Serves 10

On a flour-dusted surface, roll out the pastry thinly into a circle just larger than the size of your tart pan. Using the rolling pin to help lift it, carefully move the pastry into the pan and press it down so that it fits snugly. Trim away any excess pastry using a sharp knife, but leave some pastry hanging over the edge of the pan. This will be trimmed neatly after the tart is baked. Prick the base with a fork and chill in the refrigerator for 30 minutes.

Preheat the oven to 200°C (400°F) Gas 6.

Line the pastry with greaseproof paper, fill with baking beans and bake blind for about 15–20 minutes in the preheated oven, until the pastry is lightly golden brown. Remove the baking beans and parchment, and let cool. Turn the oven temperature down to 180°C (350°F) Gas 4.

Whisk together the eggs, sugar, lemon zest and juice, and lime juice in a bowl. Slowly pour in the cream, whisking all the time. Place in a heatproof bowl set over a pan of simmering water and heat until the mixture becomes just warm. This will take about 5 minutes.

Pour the custard into the pie crust. You may not need all of the filling, depending on the size of your pan. Bake for 30–40 minutes, until the top of the custard is lightly golden and has risen. Remove from the oven and let cool. The custard will sink back into the pie crust as it cools.

Use a sharp knife to trim away the excess pastry around the top of the pan so that the pastry is in line with the top of the tart pan. Dust with icing/confectioners' sugar to serve. This tart will keep for up to 3 days stored in the refrigerator.

Boston cream pie

Okay, okay, you don't need to say it... a Boston Cream Pie is actually a cake, not a pie. That said, a book on pies wouldn't be right without including it!

FOR THE CUSTARD FILLING

1 tablespoon cornflour/cornstarch

80 g/6½ tablespoons caster/granulated sugar

1 egg and 2 egg yolks

125 ml/generous ½ cup milk

175 ml/¾ cup double/heavy cream

1 teaspoon pure vanilla extract

FOR THE CAKE

225 g/2 sticks butter, softened

225 g/generous 1 cup caster/granulated sugar

4 eggs

225 g/1¼ cups self-raising/self-rising flour, sifted

1 teaspoon pure vanilla extract

2 tablespoons sour cream

FOR THE GANACHE

100 g/3½ oz. dark/bittersweet chocolate (70% cocoa solids)

1 tablespoon golden/light corn syrup

15 g/1 tablespoon butter

100 ml/generous ⅓ cup double/heavy cream

2 heaped tablespoons icing/confectioners' sugar, sifted

TO DECORATE

50 g/2 oz. white chocolate, melted and cooled

100 g/1¼ cups toasted flaked/slivered almonds

25-cm/10-in. springform cake pan, greased and lined

2 piping/pastry bags, one with large round nozzle/tip and one with very small round nozzle/tip

Serves 10

Begin by preparing the custard, as it needs to cool before being used to fill the cake. Whisk together the cornflour/cornstarch, sugar, egg and egg yolks, until thick, creamy and doubled in size. Place the milk, cream and vanilla into a saucepan and bring to the boil, then pour over the egg mixture in a thin stream while still hot, whisking constantly. Return the custard to the pan and whisk until thick. Take care to stir all the time and watch the custard carefully, as it can curdle easily. If the mixture starts to scramble, pass through a sieve/strainer, beating hard, and it should become smooth again. Place in a bowl and cover the surface of the custard with clingfilm/plastic wrap to prevent a skin forming. Chill in the refrigerator until needed.

Preheat the oven to 180°C (350°F) Gas 4.

For the cake, whisk together the butter and sugar in a bowl using an electric mixer until light and creamy. Add the eggs and whisk again. Fold in the flour, vanilla and sour cream until incorporated. Spoon into the cake pan. Bake in the preheated oven for 40–50 minutes, until the cake springs back to your touch and a knife comes out clean when inserted into the centre of the cake. Turn the cake out onto a rack to cool.

For the chocolate ganache, break the chocolate into pieces and place in a heatproof bowl with the syrup, butter and cream set over a saucepan of simmering water. Stir until melted and you have a thick, glossy sauce. Sift in the icing/confectioners' sugar and beat together. Let cool slightly.

Cut the cake in half and place the bottom half on a cooling rack with a sheet of foil below to catch any drips. Spoon the custard into a piping/pastry bag fitted with a large nozzle/tip and pipe the custard over the cake. Top with the second cake. Pour the warm chocolate ganache over the top of the cake and spread over the top and sides using a round-bladed knife.

Place the melted white chocolate in a piping/pastry bag fitted with a small nozzle/tip and, starting in the centre of the cake, pipe a spiral of chocolate until you reach the outside edge of the cake. Using a sharp knife, pull lines from the centre of the cake to make a feathered effect with the white chocolate. Press the almonds into the sides of the cake so that they stick to the chocolate ganache. Leave to set on the rack then, once the icing has set, slide a sharp knife underneath the cake to release it, and carefully transfer to a serving plate.

This cake will keep for up to 2 days stored in the refrigerator, but is best eaten on the day it is made.

Crème brûlée tarts

The classic French dessert of crème brûlée is always popular, and I have used that delicious sugar-topped custard to fill these delicate tarts. Make these ahead for a dinner party and simply caramelize the tops before serving.

FOR THE PIE CRUST

260 g/9 oz. digestive biscuits/graham crackers

130 g/9 tablespoons butter, melted

FOR THE FILLING

4 egg yolks

80 g/6½ tablespoons caster/granulated sugar, plus extra for sprinkling

½ teaspoon vanilla salt (or regular salt)

500 ml/generous 2 cups double/heavy cream

six 10-cm/4-in. loose-bottom, round, fluted tartlet pans, greased

chefs blow torch

Makes 6

For the pie crust, place the digestive biscuits/graham crackers in a food processor or blender and blitz to fine crumbs, or place in a clean plastic bag and bash with a rolling pin. Stir in the melted butter, ensuring that all the crumbs are well coated. Press the crumbs into the base and sides of the pans.

For the brûlée filling, whisk the egg yolks, sugar and vanilla salt until thick and creamy. Heat the cream in a saucepan and bring to the boil. Pour the hot cream over the egg mixture, whisking constantly, and then return the custard mixture to the pan. Heat gently, whisking constantly, until the mixture thickens. Take care not to overcook the custard, otherwise is will scramble.

Pour the custard into the tartlet pans and let cool, then chill in the refrigerator for 2–3 hours.

When you are ready to serve, sprinkle a little sugar over the top of each tart and then caramelize using the blow torch. Serve immediately. The uncaramelized pies will keep in the refrigerator for up to 2 days.

Scandinavian cardamom cream pie

When I was developing this recipe, I gave a slice to a delivery man who called at my house. Ten minutes later there was a knock on the door and he had returned to say it was amazing and could I sell him a whole pie? I decided that was enough of a testimony for this recipe to make it into the book!

FOR THE PIE CRUST

1 quantity shortcrust pastry (see page 9) or 500 g/18 oz. ready-made shortcrust pastry

plain/all-purpose flour, for dusting

1 egg, beaten

FOR THE FILLING

6–7 cooking apples

freshly squeezed juice of 1 lime

seeds of 8 cardamom pods

a pinch of salt

100 g/½ cup caster/granulated sugar

½ teaspoon vanilla bean powder or 1 teaspoon vanilla extract

2 eggs

500 ml/generous 2 cups sour cream

100 g/¾ cup plain/all-purpose flour

FOR THE TOPPING

150 g/generous 1 cup plain/all-purpose flour, sifted

80 g/6½ tablespoons soft dark brown sugar

80 g/¾ stick butter, chilled

20 x 30-cm/8 x 12-in. loose-bottom, fluted tart pan, greased

Serves 10

On a flour-dusted surface, roll out the pastry thinly into a circle just larger than the size of your tart pan. Using the rolling pin to help lift it, carefully move the pastry into the pan and press it down so that it fits snugly. Trim away any excess pastry using a sharp knife. Prick the base with a fork and chill in the refrigerator for 30 minutes.

Preheat the oven to 180°C (350°F) Gas 4.

Brush the base of the pastry case with some of the beaten egg using a pastry brush.

Peel and core the apples and cut into slices. Sprinkle the apples with the lime juice to prevent them from discolouring. Grind the cardamom seeds in a pestle and mortar with the salt to a fine dust, and sprinkle over the apple slices. Add the sugar and vanilla to the apples, and stir well so that the sugar is well mixed in.

Beat the eggs and sour cream together in a jug/cup and pour over the apples. Sift over the flour and then fold everything together using a spatula, so that everything is mixed well. Spoon the apple mixture into the chilled pie crust, so that the case is filled completely.

For the topping, mix the flour and sugar together, ensuring that there are no lumps of sugar. Rub the butter into the mixture with your fingertips, until the mixture resembles breadcrumbs. Sprinkle the crumble topping over the apples in a thick layer.

Bake the pie in the preheated oven for 45–60 minutes, until the apples are soft and the pastry is golden brown. I like to serve this pie cold, but it is also nice warm, if you prefer. It will keep for up to 3 days stored in the refrigerator.

Tiramisù pie

This pie is inspired by the Italian dessert tiramisù, which means 'pick-me-up' and this pie certainly does just that. I love to use coffee salt as it gives an intense flavour (it is available from good delicatessens or online). It needs to be eaten soon after being made, or the sponge will become too soft and crumbly from the alcohol.

FOR THE SPONGE BASE

170 g/1½ sticks butter, softened

170 g/generous ¾ cup caster/granulated sugar

3 eggs

170 g/1¼ cups self-raising/self-rising flour, sifted

1 teaspoon baking powder

1 shot espresso coffee

½ teaspoon coffee salt (or sea salt)

1 tablespoon sour cream

FOR THE SYRUP

4 tablespoons coffee liqueur

1 shot espresso coffee, cooled

FOR THE FILLING

250 g/generous 1 cup mascarpone cheese

250 ml/generous 1 cup crème fraîche

2 tablespoons icing/confectioners' sugar, sifted, plus extra for dusting

15 hard amaretti biscuits/cookies, crushed

80 g/3 oz. dark/bittersweet chocolate, coarsely grated

unsweetened cocoa powder, for dusting

28-cm/11-in. round tart pan with a raised centre, greased

piping/pastry bag fitted with a large star nozzle/tip

Serves 8–10

Preheat the oven to 180°C (350°F) Gas 4.

For the sponge base, cream together the butter and sugar. Add the eggs and whisk in. Add the flour, baking powder, espresso, coffee salt and sour cream. Spoon into the tart pan and bake for 20–30 minutes, until the cake springs back to your touch. Turn out onto a wire rack and leave to cool.

Mix together the coffee liqueur and espresso coffee and set aside. For the filling, whisk together the mascarpone, crème fraîche and icing/confectioners' sugar, until thick. Spoon the mixture into a piping/pastry bag fitted with a large star nozzle/tip.

Place the cake on a serving plate. Drizzle over some of the coffee syrup, until the centre of the sponge cake is covered with a light drizzle. You may not need all of the syrup. Sprinkle over one-third of the amaretti biscuit pieces and grated chocolate, and dust with a little cocoa powder and icing/confectioners' sugar.

Pipe half of the cream filling in stars over the centre of the cake. Sprinkle over a further third of the amaretti and chocolate, and dust with more cocoa powder and icing/confectioners' sugar. Next, pipe another layer of cream stars on top with the remainder of the cream, and cover with a good layer of cocoa powder and icing/confectioners' sugar dusted over the top. Decorate the top of the pie with the remaining amaretti pieces and chocolate.

This pie needs to be eaten within 4 hours of being made, otherwise the cake becomes too soft, but you can prepare the cake itself ahead of time and store in an airtight container for up to 2 days.

Portuguese custard tarts

These little tarts are one of the national treats of Portugal. They are made with a puff pastry crust and filled with a cinnamon-flavoured custard. There is much debate over the flavouring of these tarts. I have used cinnamon, vanilla and lemon, but you can use any of combination of these you prefer, simply omitting the flavours you do not wish to use.

6 egg yolks

120 g/generous ½ cup caster/granulated sugar

1 teaspoon ground cinnamon

1 teaspoon pure vanilla extract

freshly grated zest of 1 lemon

3 tablespoons plain/all-purpose flour, plus extra for dusting

200 ml/generous ¾ cup milk

150 ml/⅔ cup double/heavy cream

500 g/18 oz. puff pastry

two 12-hole muffin pans, greased

8-cm/3-in. round cookie cutter

Makes 18

In a bowl, whisk together the egg yolks, sugar, cinnamon, vanilla extract, lemon zest and flour, until the mixture is thick and creamy and has doubled in size. In a saucepan heat the milk and cream, and bring to the boil. Remove from the heat and pour over the egg mixture, whisking constantly. Return the custard to the pan and cook for a few minutes over a gentle heat, until the custard starts to thicken. Remove from the heat and cover the surface of the custard with clingfilm/plastic wrap to prevent a skin from forming. Leave to go cold.

Preheat the oven to 200°C (400°F) Gas 6.

On a flour-dusted surface, roll the puff pastry out into a large rectangle, about 30 x 20 cm/12 x 8 in. in size. Starting with one of the long sides, roll the pastry up into a long sausage shape, so that the pastry is spiralled inside. Cut the pastry into 18 slices.

Taking each slice in turn and dusting well with flour, roll each pastry disc out into a circle just larger than 8 cm/3 in., pressing down to make sure that the layers of pastry join together. Cut out a neat circle with the cutter, discarding the trimmings, and press into a hole in the muffin pan. You need the pastry to fit neatly into the hole of the muffin pan and not overhang the edges. Repeat with all the remaining pastry discs and divide the custard equally between them.

Bake each tray of tarts for 15–20 minutes, until the pastry is golden brown and the custard is set. These tarts are best eaten on the day they are made, and can be eaten warm or cold.

Kentish pudding pie

My dad loves rice pudding and this recipe is dedicated to him. Kentish pudding pie is an old English pie containing rice, fruit and spices. Although traditionally made with rice flakes, I have made this version using rice pudding, which is more easily available and is just as delicious. If you like the flavour of rice pudding then this is a pie you just have to try.

FOR THE PIE CRUST

1 quantity shortcrust pastry (see page 9) or 500 g/18 oz. ready-made shortcrust pastry

plain/all-purpose flour, for dusting

FOR THE FILLING

6 egg yolks

200 g/7 oz. sweetened condensed milk

400 ml/scant 1¾ cups double/heavy cream

1 teaspoon ground cinnamon

1 teaspoon ground mixed/apple pie spice

1 teaspoon vanilla extract

100 g/¾ cup raisins or sultanas/golden raisins

3 tablespoons store-bought rice pudding

freshly grated nutmeg

icing/confectioners' sugar, for dusting

23-cm/9-in. loose-bottom, round, fluted tart pan, greased

baking beans

Serves 10

On a flour-dusted surface, roll out the pastry thinly into a circle just larger than the size of your tart pan. Using the rolling pin to help lift it, carefully move the pastry into the pan and press it down so that it fits snugly. Trim away any excess pastry using a sharp knife, but leave some pastry hanging over the edge of the pan. This will be trimmed neatly after the tart is baked. Prick the base with a fork and chill in the refrigerator for 30 minutes.

Preheat the oven to 200°C (400°F) Gas 6.

Line the pastry with baking parchment, fill with baking beans and bake blind for about 20–25 minutes, until the pastry is golden brown. Remove the pastry case from the oven and reduce the oven temperature to 150°C (300°F) Gas 2. Remove the baking parchment and baking beans from the pie crust.

Whisk the egg yolks until light and creamy. Add the condensed milk and whisk again. Pour in the cream and add the cinnamon, mixed/apple pie spice and vanilla extract, and whisk everything together. Add the raisins, rice pudding and a grate of nutmeg, fold everything together, then pour into the pie crust. Grate a little extra nutmeg over the top of the pie and transfer carefully to the oven.

Bake for about 1–1½ hours, until the top of the pie is very lightly golden brown and set with a slight wobble. Let cool.

Use a sharp knife to trim away the excess pastry around the top of the pan so that the pastry is in line with the top of the tart pan. Dust with icing/confectioners' sugar to serve. This pie will keep for up to 3 days in the refrigerator.

Piña colada pie

This sunshine pie was inspired by my holiday to Jamaica, during which I sampled many coconut desserts and drank the occasional piña colada (or two)! Packed with exotic flavours, this is a perfect party pie.

FOR THE PIE CRUST

300 g/10½ oz. coconut biscuits/cookies

120 g/1 stick butter, melted

FOR THE FILLING

6 egg yolks

80 g/6½ tablespoons caster/granulated sugar

4 tablespoons coconut rum

250 ml/generous 1 cup double/heavy cream

150 ml/⅔ cup coconut milk

1 tablespoon melted butter

½ teaspoon vanilla bean powder or 1 teaspoon pure vanilla extract

FOR THE TOPPING

50 g/¾ cup long, shredded, sweetened coconut

1 small pineapple

4 tablespoons coconut rum

300 ml/1¼ cups double/heavy cream

23-cm/9-in. loose-bottom, round, fluted tart pan, greased

Serves 10

Blitz the biscuits/cookies to fine crumbs in a food processor or blender, or place in a clean plastic bag and bash with a rolling pin. Stir in the melted butter, ensuring that all the crumbs are coated. Press the crumbs into the base and sides of the pan.

Preheat the oven to 150°C (300°F) Gas 2.

For the filling, whisk together the egg yolks and sugar until light and creamy. Slowly pour in the rum, cream, coconut milk, melted butter and vanilla, and whisk everything together.

Wrap the base and sides of the pan in foil and place on a baking sheet to catch any butter that might be released during baking. Pour the mixture into the pie crust. Transfer carefully to the oven.

Bake for 1½ hours, until the top of the custard is very lightly golden brown and set with a slight wobble still in the centre. Let cool.

For the topping, toast the coconut in a dry frying pan/skillet over a gentle heat, until it is lightly golden brown, stirring all the time to ensure that it does not burn. Let cool.

Peel and core the pineapple and cut into small chunks. Place in a bowl and pour over the rum. Leave to soak.

Place the pie on a serving plate. Whip the cream to stiff peaks using a mixer or whisk. Spoon the cream over the coconut custard. Drain the pineapple and place on top of the cream. Sprinkle over the toasted coconut. Serve immediately, or store for up to 2 days in the refrigerator.

Holiday specials

Chocolate orange pie

Pumpkin marshmallow pie

Chocolate cinnamon pie

Pecan pie

Mincemeat tart

Eggnog pie

Pear and cranberry pie

Chocolate orange pie

Every Christmas I always find a Terry's Chocolate Orange at the bottom of my stocking — it is one of our family traditions, so the combination of chocolate and orange always brings back fond memories of Christmas morning for me. This is a rich and indulgent pie — delicate orange custard with a hidden chocolate ganache layer, all encased in a bitter chocolate crust.

FOR THE CRUST

300 g/10½ oz. chocolate sandwich cookies, such as Oreos

130 g/9 tablespoons butter, melted

2 tablespoons caster/granulated sugar

FOR THE GANACHE

100 g/3½ oz. dark/bittersweet chocolate

200 ml/scant 1 cup double/heavy cream

FOR THE ORANGE CUSTARD

9 eggs

grated zest and freshly squeezed juice of 3 small oranges

freshly squeezed juice of 1 lime

300 g/1½ cups caster/granulated sugar

300 ml/1¼ cups double/heavy cream

4 tablespoons Grand Marnier or orange liqueur

FOR THE DECORATION

30 g/1 oz. plain/semisweet chocolate, melted

23-cm/9-in. loose-bottom, round, fluted tart pan, greased

Serves 10

Blitz the cookies to fine crumbs in a food processor or blender, or place in a clean plastic bag and bash with a rolling pin. Add the melted butter and sugar, and mix well so that all the crumbs are coated in butter. Using the back of a spoon, press the cookie crumb mixture into the prepared pan so that the sides have a thick layer of crumbs to hold the filling and the base is completely covered, with no gaps.

For the ganache, break the chocolate into small pieces and place in a heatproof bowl with the cream over a pan of simmering water. Heat until the chocolate melts, then stir well so that the chocolate and cream combine and you have a thick paste. Pour the ganache into the prepared pie crust and spread out in a layer over the base of the pan. Chill in the refrigerator for 1 hour.

Preheat the oven to 180°C (350°F) Gas 4.

For the custard, whisk the eggs together until light and fluffy, then add the orange and lime juice and zest along with the sugar, and whisk well. Slowly pour in the cream and liqueur while still whisking. Place the orange custard mixture in a heatproof bowl set over a pan of simmering water and heat gently for about 5 minutes, whisking all the time, until the mixture becomes warm but not hot.

Place the chilled pie crust onto a baking sheet with some foil around the base and sides of the pan to catch any melted butter that is released from the pan during baking. Carefully pour in the orange custard mixture. You may not need it all, depending on how deep your pan is. Carefully transfer to the oven and bake for 40–50 minutes, until the custard is almost set but still has a slight wobble in the centre and is lightly golden brown on top. Remove from the oven and allow to cool. The custard layer will sink back down within the case on cooling.

When cool, decorate the top of the pie with pretty swirls of the melted plain chocolate, and leave to set before serving. This pie can be stored in the refrigerator for up to 3 days.

Pumpkin marshmallow pie

The filling for this pie has a beautiful orange colour and is the perfect treat to serve for Thanksgiving or at a Halloween party. Rich and creamy, and delicately spiced with cinnamon, nutmeg, ginger and vanilla, this pie is great served with a large spoonful of clotted or whipped cream.

FOR THE PIE CRUST

1 quantity shortcrust pastry (see page 9) or 500 g/18 oz. ready-made shortcrust pastry

plain/all-purpose flour, for dusting

FOR THE FILLING

250 g/9 oz. pumpkin purée (such as Libby's)

½ teaspoon salt

2 teaspoons ground cinnamon

½ teaspoon vanilla bean powder or 1 teaspoon pure vanilla extract

1 teaspoon ground ginger

a pinch of freshly grated nutmeg

2 tablespoons melted butter

200 g/scant 1 cup cream cheese

140 g/scant ¾ cup caster/granulated sugar

3 eggs

250 ml/generous 1 cup double/heavy cream

TO DECORATE

small and large white marshmallows

23-cm/9-in. loose-bottom, round, fluted tart pan, greased
baking beans
chef's blow torch

Serves 10

On a flour-dusted surface, roll out the pastry thinly into a circle just larger than the size of your tart pan. Using the rolling pin to help lift it, carefully move the pastry into the pan and press it down so that it fits snugly. Trim away any excess pastry using a sharp knife, but leave some pastry hanging over the edge of the pan. This will be trimmed neatly after the tart is baked. Prick the base with a fork and chill in the refrigerator for 30 minutes.

Preheat the oven to 200°C (400°F) Gas 6.

Line the pastry with baking parchment, fill with baking beans and bake blind for about 15–20 minutes in the preheated oven, until the pastry is lightly golden brown. Once cool enough to handle, remove the beans and parchment. Trim the top of the pastry case by sliding a sharp knife along the top of the pan. Turn the oven temperature down to 180°C (350°F) Gas 4.

For the filling, whisk together the pumpkin purée, salt, cinnamon, vanilla, ginger, nutmeg, melted butter, cream cheese, sugar, eggs and cream using a mixer, until you have a smooth cream. Pour the filling into the pie crust and carefully transfer to the oven.

Bake for 50–60 minutes until the custard is just set but still has a slight wobble in the centre. Let cool.

Decorate the pie with marshmallows, then use a chef's blow torch to lightly toast the tops of the marshmallows. Serve immediately. The pie will keep for up to 3 days stored in the refrigerator, but only put the marshmallows on just before serving.

Chocolate cinnamon pie

This pie is quick and easy to prepare with very minimal cooking. Chocolate and cinnamon are two flavours that instantly transport me to Christmas, and this pie is one of my favourites. If you are serving this pie for a special party and want to create a stunning centrepiece, top with cinnamon spun sugar and glittering gold leaf that will twinkle in the candlelight.

FOR THE PIE CRUST

300 g/10½ oz. chocolate sandwich cookies, such as Oreos

125 g/9 tablespoons butter, melted

FOR THE CHOCOLATE CINNAMON FILLING

2 eggs

375 ml/generous 1½ cups double/heavy cream

125 ml/generous ½ cup milk

300 g/10½ oz. dark/bittersweet chocolate, minimum 70% cocoa solids, broken into pieces

2 teaspoons ground cinnamon

FOR THE CINNAMON SPUN SUGAR

100 g/½ cup caster/ superfine sugar

1 teaspoon ground cinnamon

edible gold leaf

23-cm/9-in. loose-bottom, round fluted tart pan, greased

Serves 10

For the pie crust, blitz the cookies to fine crumbs in a food processor or blender, or place in a clean plastic bag and bash with a rolling pin. Stir in the melted butter, ensuring that all the crumbs are well coated. Using the back of a spoon, press the cookie crumb mixture into the prepared pan so that the sides have a thick layer of crumbs to hold the filling and the base is completely covered, with no gaps.

For the filling, whisk the eggs, cream and milk together. Place the chocolate pieces in a saucepan with the cream mixture and the cinnamon. Heat over a gentle heat, stirring all the time, for about 4–5 minutes, until the chocolate is melted and the ganache is thick and glossy. Pour into the pie crust and chill in the refrigerator for several hours or, ideally, overnight.

When you are ready to serve, prepare the cinnamon spun sugar. Place the sugar and ground cinnamon in a heavy-based saucepan over a gentle heat. Heat until the sugar has melted and turns a light golden brown. Do not stir the pan with a spoon, but swirl it to keep the sugar moving. Take care towards the end of cooking, as the sugar can burn easily. Remove from the heat and leave to cool for about 1 minute, until the sugar thickens slightly.

Using a fork, spin fine threads of sugar over the top of the pie to create a 'net' effect. Add small pieces of gold leaf to the sugar to decorate. Once topped with the spun sugar, the pie needs to be served immediately, as the sugar will become sticky in contact with the air. This pie will keep – without the spun sugar – in the refrigerator for up to 3 days.

Pecan pie

Pecan pie is one of the most popular pies – certainly in America, from where it originates. It can be served for Thanksgiving as an alternative to pumpkin pie. I have added hints of orange to this pie, which works well with the cinnamon.

FOR THE PIE CRUST

115 g/1 stick butter, chilled

280 g/generous 2 cups plain/ all-purpose flour, sifted, plus extra for dusting

40 g/3¼ tablespoons caster/ granulated sugar

2 egg yolks

grated zest of 1 orange

1 teaspoon vanilla bean powder or seeds of ½ vanilla pod/bean

FOR THE FILLING

400 g/3½ cups pecan halves

150 g/¾ cup caster/ granulated sugar

150 g/¾ cup muscovado/ molasses sugar

2 teaspoons ground cinnamon

½ teaspoon vanilla salt (or ½ teaspoon regular salt plus 1 teaspoon pure vanilla extract)

freshly squeezed juice of 1 small orange

100 g/7 tablespoons butter

400 g/1⅓ cup golden/ light corn syrup

3 eggs, beaten

23-cm/9-in. loose-bottom, round, fluted tart pan, greased

Serves 10

For the pastry, rub the butter into the flour with your fingertips. Add the sugar, egg yolks, orange zest and vanilla, and bring together into a soft dough, adding 1–2 tablespoons of cold water if needed. Wrap the pastry in clingfilm/plastic wrap and chill for 30 minutes in the refrigerator.

On a flour-dusted surface, roll out the pastry thinly into a circle just larger than the size of your tart pan. Using the rolling pin to help lift it, carefully move the pastry into the pan and press it down so that it fits snugly. Trim away any excess pastry using a sharp knife, but leave some pastry hanging over the edge of the pan. This will be trimmed neatly after the tart is baked. Prick the base with a fork and chill in the refrigerator for 30 minutes.

Preheat the oven to 180°C (350°F) Gas 4.

Reserve about 18 pecan halves for decoration. Blitz the remaining nuts to fine crumbs in the food processor and pour into the chilled pie crust. Heat the caster/granulated and muscovado/molasses sugars, cinnamon, salt, orange juice, butter and golden/light corn syrup in a saucepan over a gentle heat, until the sugar and butter have melted. Let cool slightly.

Whisk the eggs into the syrup. Pass the syrup through a sieve/ strainer and pour most of the syrup over the pecans, reserving a little for glazing. Mix the nuts and syrup lightly with a fork. Place the reserved pecan halves on top of the pie to decorate.

Bake for 25 minutes, then turn the temperature down to 150°C (300°F) Gas 2 and bake for a further 10–15 minutes, until the pie is set but still has a slight wobble in the centre. Remove from the oven. Trim the edge of the pastry to the level of the pan using a sharp knife. Reheat the reserved syrup and brush over the top of the pie to glaze. Let cool before serving. Store for up to 3 days in an airtight container.

Mincemeat tart

This festive tart is covered with a pretty snowflake top. The mincemeat has a hidden cream-cheese layer which acts as creamy balance to the sharp mincemeat. The tart keeps well, so is a great standby at Christmas for unexpected visitors.

FOR THE PIE CRUST

1 quantity shortcrust pastry (see page 9) or 500 g/18 oz. ready-made shortcrust pastry

plain/all-purpose flour, for dusting

1 egg, beaten

caster/granulated sugar, for sprinkling

FOR THE FILLING

800 g/3½ cups mincemeat

150 g/²/₃ cup cream cheese

grated zest of 1 large orange

1 teaspoon ground cinnamon

FOR THE DECORATION

icing/confectioners' sugar, for dusting

35 x 10-cm/14 x 4-in. loose-bottom, rectangular tart pan, greased

small snowflake cutters

Serves 8

Divide the pastry in half and, on a flour-dusted surface, roll out half into a rectangle just larger than the size of your pan. Press into the base and sides of the pan. Brush the pastry with some of the beaten egg.

Place half of the mincemeat into the pie crust and spread out into an even layer. Place small spoonfuls of the cream cheese over the mincemeat. Sprinkle the orange zest and ground cinnamon over the cream cheese. Top with the remaining mincemeat and spread out evenly.

Roll out the remaining pastry into a rectangle just larger than the size of your pan. Cut out small snowflakes in the pastry in a pretty pattern, reserving the cut-out snowflakes for decoration. Using a rolling pin to help lift, place the pastry on top of the tart. Crimp together the top and bottom pastry layers, trimming the edge of the pastry as necessary. Brush the top of the tart with some beaten egg to glaze, then decorate with the reserved snowflakes, brushing the tops of them with a little beaten egg as well. Sprinkle with a little caster/granulated sugar.

Bake in the oven for 35–40 minutes, until golden brown, then remove from the oven and let cool.

The tart will keep for up to 3 days stored in an airtight container. Serve warm or cold with brandy butter or brandy custard.

Eggnog pie

This festive little pie is inspired by the popular holiday-season drink "eggnog". The custard is flavoured with warming cinnamon, nutmeg and vanilla, and, to me, tastes of the spirit of Christmas.

FOR THE PIE CRUST

300 g/10½ oz. digestive biscuits/ graham crackers

125 g/9 tablespoons butter, melted

FOR THE FILLING

300 g/1⅓ cups cream cheese

300 ml/1¼ cups sour cream

2 eggs

4 tablespoons dark rum

1 heaped teaspoon ground cinnamon

½ teaspoon ground mixed/ apple pie spice

a pinch of freshly grated nutmeg

50 g/¼ cup soft dark brown sugar

50 g/¼ cup caster/ granulated sugar

a pinch of salt

23-cm/9-in. loose-bottom, round, fluted tart pan, greased

Serves 10

For the pie crust, place the biscuits/crackers in a food processor or blender and blitz to fine crumbs or place in a clean plastic bag and bash with a rolling pin. Stir in the melted butter, ensuring that all the crumbs are well coated. Press the crumbs into the base and sides of the pan.

Preheat the oven to 170°C (325°F) Gas 3.

For the filling, whisk together the cream cheese, sour cream, eggs, rum, cinnamon, mixed/apple pie spice, nutmeg, soft dark brown sugar, caster/granulated sugar and salt, until smooth and creamy.

Wrap the base and sides of the pan in foil, then place the tart pan on a large baking sheet and pour in the filling. Grate a little extra nutmeg over the top of the pie.

Bake in the preheated oven for 50–60 minutes, until the filling is set but still has a slight wobble in the centre. Let cool before serving with whipped cream, flavoured with a little extra rum if you choose. This pie will store for up to 3 days in the refrigerator.

Pear and cranberry pie

Cranberries and pears are a great combination, and this festive pie decorated with stars and snowflakes is a comforting treat and a good alternative to other rich desserts often eaten in the holiday season. You can use frozen or dried cranberries if fresh cranberries are not available.

FOR THE PIE CRUST

1 quantity shortcrust pastry (see page 9) or 500 g/18 oz. ready-made shortcrust pastry

plain/all-purpose flour, for dusting

1 egg, beaten

FOR THE FILLING

10 ripe pears

freshly squeezed juice of 1 lemon

150 g/generous 1½ cups fresh cranberries

2 teaspoons ground cinnamon

150 g/¾ cup caster/granulated sugar, plus extra for sprinkling

2 tablespoons plain/all-purpose flour, plus extra for dusting

a pinch of salt

60 g/½ stick butter, cubed

23-cm/9-in. round pie dish, greased

snowflake and star cutters

Serves 8

Preheat the oven to 200°C (400°F) Gas 6.

Divide the pastry in half and, on a flour-dusted surface, roll out half into a circle just larger than the size of your pie dish. Press into the pan and brush the inside of the pastry with some of the beaten egg using a pastry brush.

For the filling, peel and core the pears and cut into slices. Place in a bowl and toss in the lemon juice to prevent the pears from discolouring. Add the cranberries, cinnamon, sugar, flour and salt, and toss together with your hands so everything is well mixed. Place the fruit mixture into the pastry case and dot the top of the fruit with the cubes of butter.

Brush the outer edge of the lower pastry case with a little of the beaten egg. Roll out the remaining pastry into a circle just larger than the size of your pie dish and place over the apples. Crimp together the pastry by pinching between your fingers. Trim away any excess pastry. You can reroll this out and cut out snowflakes and stars to decorate the top of your pie if you wish. Cut a slit in the centre of the pie to let any steam escape. Brush the top of the pie and the pastry decorations with a little more egg and sprinkle with caster/granulated sugar.

Bake in the preheated oven for 25 minutes, then reduce the temperature to 170°C (350°F) Gas 4 and bake for about 35 minutes more, until the pie is golden brown and the fruit is soft. Remove from the oven and let cool for about 15 minutes, then serve straight away with custard or cream. This pie is best eaten on the day it is made, but can be stored for up to 2 days in the refrigerator.

Index

Acknowledgments

Heartfelt thanks to Ryland Peters and Small for publishing this book – especially Julia Charles for commissioning the book and being such a fab friend, Kate Eddison for her unending patient editing, Leslie Harrington and David Hearn for the wonderful design and production, and Lauren Wright for her fabulous PR support. To Steve Painter, Lucy McKelvie and Cherry Ackerman, as always you took my recipes and created such stunning pictures – I am so grateful to you all. Love and thanks to Heather, Elly and Jack of HHB agency. To my Mum and Dad, thanks for always being there – you mean the world to me. To my friends – Michelle, Dave, Ann, Christina, Karen, Amanda, Heather, Gav, Rachel, Damon, all at Brightside Roofing, Fay, Harry, Jake, Chris, Clare, Russ, Charlotte, Dan, David, Lucy, Miles, Jess, Joshua Pickle, Rosie Pea, Alison, Ella, Torin, Maren, Justina, Pam and the members of WOAC – thank you all for going beyond the call of duty and consuming so much pie!

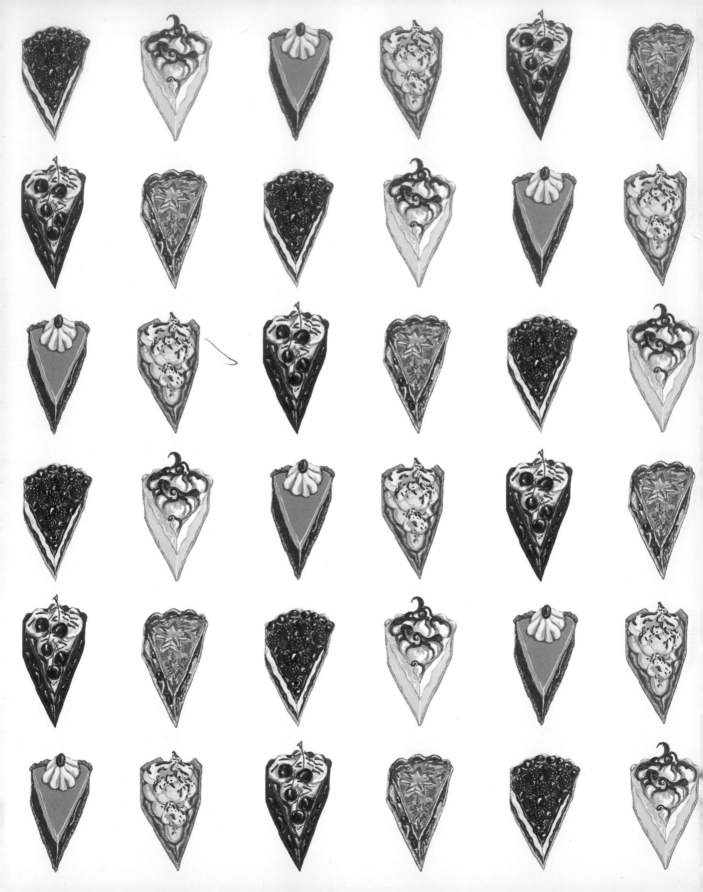